M000015368

"Many marital relationships are shattered when one of the partners transitions gender roles. Despite all obstacles, this marriage, thanks to long and hard work by both partners, endures. This is an inspirational book that pulls no punches."

— Dallas Denny, writer, transgender activist,
creator of *Chrysalis Quarterly* magazine

"A compelling and captivating tale of love, compassion, understanding, and commitment. A beautiful piece of literature that tells a powerful true story of an ordinary couple weathering extraordinary circumstances."

— Dr. Ronald Holt, psychiatrist, speaker,
and best-selling author of *PRIDE*

"This incredible book tells an amazing story that will make you feel happy, angry, eager, sad, and even helpless at times. You are taken on a journey and will completely succumb to both the individual and collective emotions of a couple's authentic love story. It not only emphasizes how one's transition affects more than the transitioner, but it attacks the societal perception of what 'normal' is. Any and every one can find comfort in this book."

— Rena Ingram, founder of FreedomTwoLove
and motivational speaker

www.mascotbooks.com

Who Am I If You're Not You?

For more information, please contact:
Mascot Books
560 Herndon Parkway #120
Herndon, VA 20170
info@mascotbooks.com

CPSIA Code: PROPM0917A
Library of Congress Control Number: 2017911085
ISBN-13: 978-1-68401-474-3

Printed in the United States

love's journey *beyond* gender

who
am i
if you're
not you?

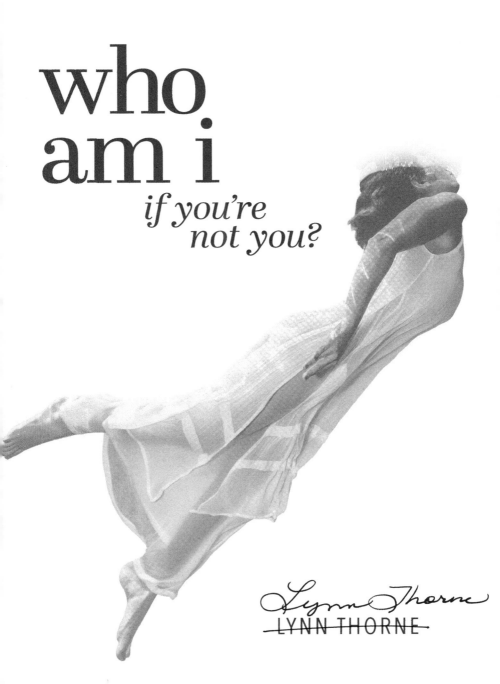

Lynn Thorne
LYNN THORNE

Foreword

Dr. Jennifer Leggour

The story of Jennifer and Marc—the real-life couple at the heart of *Who Am I If You're Not You?*—is very familiar to me. I treated Jen and shared her experience as she watched her partner undergo a life-changing transformation. Marc was not the only one who transformed; Jen was also challenged to re-identify herself. This was a painful process with grief, self-destruction, and questionable hope. Jen never gave up on herself or Marc, and worked diligently to create a life worth living. In her healing process, she came to a place of acceptance and peace. I like to use the analogy of a butterfly metamorphosis, going from caterpillar to chrysalis to butterfly. This is a fragile process with a great vulnerability; fortunately, in this case it yields a beautiful outcome. Jen and Marc are living proof of that beautiful outcome because of their hard work, dedication, and love for each other.

Who Am I If You're Not You? allows the reader to experience first-hand what unique challenges lie within a couple faced with sexual identity issues. Most often, this information is private or confidential and only helping professionals are aware. This book provides the opportunity for anyone to become informed and inspired by the courage it takes to be "your true self."

Working in the mental health field for 20 years, I have had the privilege of sharing personal and intimate parts of peoples' lives, both good and bad. I have learned that the human experience is sometimes not an easy one; however, I am instilled with hope by having seen tremendous resilience in people of all ages. This is no exception for the lesbian, gay, bi-sexual, and transgendered (LGBT) community, where life's journey can be especially difficult. This population not only struggles with their own personal journey to find identity, but does it in a world where they are often ostracized for doing so.

As a psychologist, I have worked with children, teens, and adults impacted by LGBT issues. To name a few: the four-year old boy who insists he is a girl in the wrong body; the teen girl who is romantically attracted to other teen boys and girls and is scared to tell anyone; and the adult female lesbian whose partner identified herself as transgendered and wants to become a male. What I have observed is that being LGBT is an orientation that is neither chosen nor pathological. People are born this way and are challenged to be brave enough to accept themselves while living in a society that is not often accepting of them. The statistics are true in that there are high rates of depression and suicide related to emotional shame and learned beliefs that they are "flawed, don't fit in, unworthy, unlovable, and not good enough."

I am happy to help fight the stigma that is associated with being LGBT and attest that this community of people is human like everyone else and shares the common thread of the emotional experience. They are not diseased, abnormal, rebellious, sinners, sociopathic, or crazy. An important foundation in therapy is being non-judgmental, unconditional, and empathic. Teaching coping, acceptance, and self-love are critical. I have never created a treatment plan that has aimed to change a person into being heterosexual. I encourage all members of society to adopt a similar stance and not be afraid to embrace anyone who is different in sexual orientation or otherwise.

Let this book inspire you with its story about the human experience. I know I certainly was inspired by it, and am honored to have played a part in the story it tells.

Author's Note

~~This is a true story.~~ This is a true love story.

The people in this book are real. In fact, I'm honored to say they're friends of mine. And I'm incredibly, deeply humbled, because they shared their very personal, very intimate story with me so I could share it with you.

I couldn't help but write this book. It truly, honestly, wasn't a choice. The compulsion was undeniable.

Why?

Because I believe in love. Always have. True, lasting, fairytale love that stands the test of time. Some might think that sounds foolish. Naïve. And I might've agreed with them up to a point. Sure, the divorce rate is rising all the time. That would be a good indication that my theory of true love is, perhaps, exaggerated.

But when I met Jennifer and Marc and heard their story, I was more convinced than ever that when you love someone to their very core, when you love their very *essence*, love wins.

That's what this story is about. You might think it's about gender transition. You might think it's about mental illness. You might have picked it up to read it because you thought it would be a juicy, up-close-and-personal look at a woman becoming a man. I won't lie; it is all of those things. It also includes resentment. Disappointment. Anger. And grief—the kind that exposes itself in the most unexpected ways.

You see, grief isn't reserved for death though that's when it is usually expressed. But it isn't solely reserved for the time when a soul is no longer earthbound. In this story of the couple next door, the pair grieves throughout much of their relationship: for the future they'd dreamt of, for the loss of a spouse who isn't dead, for the plans they'd made together that would never see the light of day. There's plenty of grief to go around.

But there's also hope. Life-affirming, joyous hope that sometimes flickers like a candle nearly snuffed out by a breeze but lights again from within to generate heat, light, warmth. That kind of hope.

There are many people who can benefit from this book. I didn't write it for any one particular audience. It'd be obvious to think it's written for the transgender community. Or anyone who identifies as LGBTQ+. But there are messages within that will also resonate with anyone who listens for them. Messages of inclusion. Acceptance. Strength. Perseverance. Loss. Lessons. And love. There it is again—love.

And let's not forget courage. It takes a hell of a lot of guts to become your authentic self, knowing that the majority of the world doesn't understand and that a small minority will outright ostracize you for it. Add to that the fearlessness it takes to then share your deeply personal story with the world—especially when that story is likely to draw the ire of people who believe your lifestyle is dirty, wrong, or damned—and as far as I'm concerned, these friends are among the most courageous people I know.

Writing this book has helped me learn and grow in ways I could never have imagined before I began it. I've always been an ally to the lesbian and gay community. I knew they, as a whole, had a difficult time fitting in, being accepted, feeling comfortable. People can be horrible and nasty and judgmental, and I've always wondered why gays and lesbians were so ostracized over something as simple (and private) as their sexual preference. *"Who the hell cares?"* was always my motto. But while I felt badly for them, it didn't affect me personally in any way. I went about my straight life not giving it too much thought.

I thought about the trans community even less. I wasn't aware that I knew anyone who was transgender. I'd known a couple of drag queens, but they didn't live their everyday life as the opposite sex, so what I saw was what they put forward—a performance in which they pretended to be women.

Then I met Jennifer, who told me her husband was transgender before I'd had a chance to meet him, which made me very curious when I was first introduced to him. (I tried not to stare but I was kind of weirdly fascinated, I'm sorry to say. I'd like to be able to tell you it didn't faze me at all, but that would be a lie.)

I studied Marc (nonchalantly, I'd like to think), wondering whether I'd be able to tell he'd been born female if I hadn't already known. And the answer was no; I wouldn't have guessed. And then I chastised myself—what difference did it make? I liked him. I *genuinely* liked him. He was funny and nice and a good guy. After that first meeting, he was just Marc. I didn't think about his transition much until I started writing this book, after he shared his backstory with me. It forced me to think very thoroughly about what it would be like to be born in the wrong body. I tried to put myself in his shoes … to imagine what it would feel like to have my mind not match my body. Considering it was disorienting to say the least.

Learning about Marc's experience was only one part of writing this book. Of course I also did lots of research. I learned so much about the trans community, which is more than ten million strong in the U.S. and growing. I learned that between 30–45% of transgender people have attempted suicide. I researched support groups and resources that could help them. Thanks to Marc and his willingness to tell me the most intimate details of his life, these people aren't just numbers to me anymore—no longer nameless, faceless humans. I understand (granted, in a very small way) some of the struggles they face *every day of their lives*. How horrible to feel like you can't ever be yourself. How gut-wrenchingly sad to fear the possible repercussions if you tried. And how utterly lonely to feel that the world at-large will never understand you, regardless.

That's only part of what I learned from writing this book. I also came to understand that it's never just one person who transitions. When someone decides to undergo gender reassignment, everyone around them is affected in some way—family, friends, co-workers. Even if it just means remembering to call someone a different name or use another pronoun to refer to them, ripple effects extend far beyond the person who's physically undergoing the change.

While I love to think everyone could get something out of reading this book, I know it won't appeal to everyone. There are some who will condemn its pages (and me, for writing them) simply because they choose not to understand. Others might shake their heads at it, believing those who are transgender are just going through a phase that'll pass like saggy jeans or the man bun. Despite the naysayers, Jennifer and Marc are willing to tell their story anyway—raw, personal details that for some, probably just add fuel to the fire. I'm not writing this book for those few. I'm writing it for everyone else—for those who are willing to read it, who are open to learning and better understanding. I don't expect it to change anyone's mind, but I'm hopeful it can at least open a few hearts along the way.

Because at the core of it all, that's what keeps us going. Our hearts. Our love. Our belief that love sustains us.

This story is proof.

"Some people don't understand the promises they're making when they make them."

"Right, of course. But you keep the promise anyway. That's what love is. Love is keeping the promise anyway."

— **John Green**
The Fault in Our Stars

This book is dedicated to every child who felt that they didn't fit in, who worried about being weird, or who was told they were. It's for every kid who went home crying because they felt different.

It's also dedicated to every grownup for whom that feeling never really went away, who still thinks somewhere deep inside that they've simply learned how to act the part and that "normal" is for other people.

It's not. There is no normal. There're only assumptions of what normal should look like.

This book is for the weirdos, the outcasts, and the misfits. In other words, it's for every damn one of us. Because each of us is special. Unique. One of a kind.

Which means we can't possibly be normal. We're all extraordinary.

Prologue

They lug the last box through the door, exhausted, aching, and sweaty. High fives all around, toasts to the new house, and to happy memories yet to be made there. Friends clink plastic cups of soda and water while a few enjoy the cold wash of beer down their throats after their labor. There are the expected jokes about being too old for this, even though most of them are in their early 30s and don't have a clue what being old is all about. The air is warm but comfortably so, allowing them to relax for a bit and celebrate a moving day without any major hiccups, injuries, or breakages. But soon they all drift off one by one, offering hugs and help with unpacking. At last, it is just the three of them left. They are home.

The new house is a huge milestone, as it should be. Homey, comfortable, with room to spread out, a change after the cramped apartment they just vacated. A decent yard that's big enough for privacy but not too much to maintain, partly shaded for those sweltering summer days. The porch that offers a taste of time gone by. He thinks about where to plug in the gaming stations so the cords will reach; she's focused on whether the baby could squeeze through the porch railings. You see an all-American family excited about their future. Father, mother, baby boy. Their reality looks like any Hallmark movie.

But how did that film become our everyday expectation of traditional life? Who sets the stage for what normal is *supposed* to look like? The script plays out time and again, generation after generation. Boy meets girl. They fall in love. They pledge their lives to each other. There's a baby or three who completes their family: living proof of the legacy they'll leave. And a home, always some sort of home. A cozy nest to call their own.

That's where Jennifer and Marc are right now. Home.

The next few months will find them making it their own. Of course, the big stuff is easy. Couch on that wall, love seat over there. Bed goes here because of the window. That all gets put in place pretty quickly. Then comes the more laborious part. A whole lot of boxes marked in "kitchen" in her neat penmanship, every one of them carefully packed and full of the utensils they've been convinced they can't live without but rarely use. Whisks and sauté pans, cake knives and juicers. More Tupperware than anyone could ever use (but at least every container had a lid, Jen made sure of that) is tidily stacked away. Spices and glasses and forks all found their space in cupboards and drawers in fairly short order.

In the meantime, there's everyday life. Jobs and daycare drop offs. The biting phase of every two-year-old who can't quite figure out his emotions, so he sinks his teeth in to let his feelings out. The date night for a friend's wedding. The maintenance appointment for the car. It all goes on, just as always.

From every angle looking in, they are a perfect family settling in to their new life on Water Street. But peel back a layer and you'll catch a quick glimpse of something quite different: old photos of a little girl who doesn't exist anymore but bears an uncanny resemblance to Marc. Dig just a tiny bit deeper and, surprise, there's a needle in bathroom (safely out of the baby's reach—they both make sure of that). There's the serum in the medicine cabinet at the ready for his next dose. And when the light hits her arm just right, you can see the scars, a small series of them lined up like matchsticks.

What you see from all the angles is still true. It's not a mirage, and it's certainly not a façade. They are, indeed, a sweet family filled with love, laughter, and memories in the making. But what's not so easily seen—what isn't at all obvious—is what got them to this place. Those who see this contented little trio in their first home don't know that Jen and Marc, stars of this would-be Hallmark movie, very nearly never made it at all.

Because a bomb ripped their lives apart. A verbal kind of bomb, of course, but one that was every bit as catastrophic as the kind that leaves physical wreckage scattered for miles.

And irony of ironies, it came on Valentine's Day... a "gift" Jennifer never saw coming and almost never recovered from.

Chapter 1
Valentine's Day and Other Surprises

"Damn," Marika said, as the ground beef splattered on her hand, the hot grease stinging her skin as the stove made it sizzle in the pan. She was running behind (as usual), trying to get dinner ready before Jennifer got home from work. The small but functional kitchen size meant she didn't have to go far to grab something from the fridge or a plate to put it on. The garlic and onion she added seasoned the hamburger, their scents wafted through the kitchen. The winter sun—watery and wan—warned that afternoon was short lived, the daylight all but gone. Marika flipped on a light to compensate for the encroaching darkness.

She returned to food prep. Turning down the heat on the stove, she turned her attention to the salad. Nervous energy made her jittery; she dropped the head of lettuce and had to go wash it off before starting to slice it up, the cool water easing the sting where the grease had scalded her. She'd picked up heart-shaped chocolate cupcakes for dessert on her way home, and they sat on the counter looking like a baking advertisement. The entree she was fixing wasn't fancy (Hamburger Helper's best), but it suited both of them just fine. As newlyweds they didn't have much, but they had each other. It was more than enough.

Of course, this wasn't just any meal; it was Valentine's Day. While they didn't make a big deal out of this commercial holiday, it *was* their first married Valentine's, and Marika enjoyed making dinner for her bride. Tonight had a lot riding on it that had nothing to do with the date on the calendar, and Marika wanted it to go well. She tried to focus as she sliced a cucumber, splitting through the crisp skin with a satisfying *thwack*, but her thoughts remained as scattered as the birdseed on the nearby poultry farms on Maryland's Eastern Shore.

"Hey babe," Jennifer called, as she walked through the door of the four-bedroom house they were renting from Marika's parents. "God, I'm glad to be home. And I'm starving."

Jen worked in a cardiologist's office, manning the front desk. Days were predictable, but long. Still, she was happy in her job, happy in her life, and happiest of all to be married to the woman she loved.

"Dinner will be ready in about ten," Marika said, pulling Jen in close and giving her a long hello kiss. She inhaled her wife's scent as she did so, the familiar blend of shampoo and soap instantly soothing her jangled nerves.

"Mmmm. Hi," Jen responded. She felt like the luckiest woman alive. She brushed Marika's hair back behind her ear so she could give her a follow-up kiss on the cheek. "Let me just go change," she said.

"Love ya just the way you are!" Marika teased, turning back to the tomatoes on the counter that awaited her attention.

Jen called back over her shoulder, "Love you more!" and went to switch out of her work clothes into her standard hanging-out attire—sweats and a T-shirt. Not the most romantic outfit she could've chosen, but Marika wouldn't care. They were both more focused on comfort than fashion.

Dinner was served with a side of small talk, both of them chatting about work. Jen shared stories about her newly engaged colleague at the cardiologists', Marika talked about the on-air snafu during today's shift at the local radio station where she DJ'd the midday shift. Jen didn't notice the underlying energy at the table. She was reminded how grateful she was to have a partner who liked to cook.

"This tastes really good, babe. Thanks for making it."

Marika smiled. "Happy Valentine's Day. I love you."

"Love you, too!" They toasted, each smiling at just how fortunate they felt to have found one another.

Marika had put candles on the table, and in the dim light, one almost wouldn't notice the mismatched holders they were in. Not that it would've mattered much to the couple. Money was tight, but love was free and that mattered more than matching candleholders.

It was a seemingly uneventful evening. They cleared the dishes together, stopping now and again for a kiss or a loving swat on the backside. *I hope this never changes*, Jennifer thought, as she watched her wife blow out the candles on the table.

"Hey, I have something we can watch tonight," Marika said.

"Did you get a movie?" Jen tried to imagine what she would've picked for them to watch on Valentine's night. Marika loved all genres from horror to anime, and Jen never knew what to expect. She often fell asleep before they were over anyway so it didn't really matter. She didn't push for an answer tonight, just followed Marika into the sparsely furnished guest room. They were painting their master bedroom before the new furniture arrived—the first furnishings they'd purchased together for their first home. Meantime, the guest room had become their makeshift movie theater.

They curled up on the mattress on the floor, lit only by the light from the computer screen as they watched the opening credits flicker in front of them. Jen's cat, Holly, lay down next to her, purring. Not to be outdone, the dog nestled in between them, waiting for belly rubs. They were the picture of bliss: a loving couple sharing a quiet night together. But that would all change over the next 60 minutes as the movie they watched opened up a Pandora's box that couldn't be closed again.

Chapter 2
Expectations

"You feel like you're supposed to be a man?" Jen asked the question almost inaudibly, unable to comprehend what that meant.

Both women were in shadow after the film finished. The moon and clouds played peekaboo outside. Lunar light filtered through the blinds teasing her exhausted mind. Like a wave crashing onto shore, pain submerged everything.

They were still on the mattress: two bodies next to each other that couldn't have felt any farther apart. Jen sat upright, arms hugging her knees—tight, closed off, impenetrable. Marika faced her full-on, both her posture and her heart open to sharing this most vulnerable moment. There was no sound. Some silences are as comforting as a hot cup of tea on a rainy day; this silence was agonizing as Jennifer tried to corral her thoughts into something resembling cohesion, and Marika had tried to anticipate what Jen would say next.

Jen tried again, her voice only a little louder now. "Why did you want me to watch this? Are you telling me something? Is this how you feel?"

"Yeah, I do," Marika answered without hesitation. It was a relief to have shared her thoughts at last. But with that relief came uncertainty over how Jen would react.

"Do you just relate to it? Like, this makes sense to you?" Jennifer paused, not sure she wanted to go on. Marika picked at the fringe of the blanket she'd thrown over them before the movie started. She pulled the tassels taut, feeling their velvety softness slip through her fingers before letting them fall to the mattress below. The throw that offered warmth before the movie started now felt stifling, almost as suffocating as the room. She had wanted to tell Jennifer how she felt for a couple of months but had never settled on how to break the news.

Like there's really a right way to do this, Marika thought. But still she probably should've found a different way, and maybe Valentine's Day wasn't the very best time. She'd had always been horrible at waiting, and even worse at timing things. Why should this be different? At least she'd gotten it over with.

The silence screamed in Jennifer's head. The last of the closing credits scrolled up and the computer screen had gone completely dark, blackening the room and echoing the tension.

When Jen next spoke, anxiety overshadowed her tone. She couldn't stop the questions. They were forming in her mind and spilling from her mouth almost simultaneously. "Is this just a, 'Hey, Jen, thought you'd be interested in knowing more about me' kind of thing? Or do you feel like you need to do something to change yourself?" Jen nearly choked out those last two words, "change yourself." She was compelled to ask the question but was terrified of the answer.

"I don't know," Marika responded. "I'm really not sure."

The documentary Marika had asked Jen to watch was "Gender Rebel," a film about physical and social gender transition. It detailed three biological females who felt more like men. One of them, Kimberly Ann Sallans, underwent a gender reassignment to become Ryan Sallans. His story in particular had struck a chord somewhere deep inside Marika's soul.

When Marika had seen the film a few weeks ago, it felt like the missing piece she'd been searching for. She'd never been comfortable in her own skin but hadn't known why. She just knew she had never felt that her brain and body were in sync.

Her friend from high school had recommended the movie. One night at his apartment, they were discussing why Marika perpetually felt out of place within her own body.

Tom was the first one to mention the term "gender queer," a phrase that suggests someone's gender and self-identity may be mismatched. Tom had explained, "Someone can be born a woman but really feel like a man, or the other way around." That she could've been born with a male-oriented mind but a female body suddenly made perfect sense to Marika—and had simultaneously electrified her.

Once Marika watched "Gender Rebel," the film put everything into perspective for her. Marika now knew she suffered from gender dysphoria but that night, she only knew that she'd found an answer to a question she'd had her whole life. The answer was clear. She'd been meant to be a man.

Eager to share her revelation with Jennifer, Marika wanted Jennifer to understand too. Now she wasn't so sure she'd made the right call.

Marika tried to continue the discussion. "What're you thinking?"

Jen just shook her head.

"I'm sorry I didn't time this better," Marika joked. "You know that's not a strong point of mine. Remember when I got your ring and I couldn't wait to propose so I asked you that night!?"

But Jennifer had shut down, unwilling (or unable) to hear any more. It wasn't a matter of not caring; she needed time to process what she'd just heard.

How could she feel this way? Jen thought, miserably. Thoughts spiraled from there. *How long has she felt like this? Did she know before we got married?*

Jen thought back to the day just six months ago when they looked into each other's eyes and said, "I do." The simple beach ceremony had suited them so well. A small number of family and friends looked on as sand and surf provided an idyllic background. Her mother had read a poem Jen had chosen that seemed to capture their love perfectly. The weather was ideal, sun shining down on two soul mates as they pledged to spend their lives together. They'd both seen the glorious weather as a wedding gift: a beautiful day for a perfect union. It didn't matter that it hadn't been legally recognized; in their eyes, they were together for life.

Her thoughts skipped around like a CD on shuffle mode. Promises made. Plans laid out. A future anticipated. She flashed on the many times they'd talked about having a family. Marika had joked about how much fun they'd have being parents; Jen had pictured them as two moms taking their child to the zoo and the park. They'd discussed how and when they'd tell their child why he or she was lucky enough to have two mommies and no daddy. They'd talked about baby names and nursery themes even before the wedding. And now *this!*

She couldn't reconcile it. She felt duped. Had Marika intentionally misled her?

*****

Jennifer stayed on that mattress for a long time after the film ended, crying silent tears. The serenity of the sweet family scene just an hour before splintered into a million pieces of jagged glass—each cutting Jen with shards of disbelief, incomprehension, bewilderment.

She turned in early. Lying alone in the bed they normally shared, Jennifer cocooned into a fetal position as though protecting herself from any more pain. Sleep resisted her for hours. When it had finally arrived, it was disjointed and disturbed. There had been no merciful rest. No restorative slumber. And though she'd prayed for it, no miraculous reset of the previous night's events. Opening her eyes on Thursday morning, Jen felt her whole world crash down on her all over again.

*****

Jennifer drove to the office as rain pelted the windshield. She couldn't get the wipers adjusted to keep up with the volume. It was either too slow and rain blurred her vision or too fast and squeaked every other swipe. She was grateful to get out of the damp weather and start her day, hoping that work would offer a beacon of normalcy. Walking into the office, she did her best to pretend nothing was different.

"Good morning, sunshine!" Amber said from the front desk.

"Hey." Jen tried to manage a smile.

"Wet out there, isn't it?"

"Yeah. Good day to stay in bed." *For more than one reason*, Jen thought. Some days she stopped and chatted with Amber for a minute on her way to her desk. Today she hurried past, hoping not to get caught up in small talk.

The familiar setting offered no solace. She felt like she was trying to run waist deep in the ocean: torment chased her and she wasn't fast enough to escape it. Just yesterday her world had been brightly brimming with possibilities. Today that same world seemed void of color. Lost and frightened, Jennifer felt her life had been turned upside down. Righting it seemed impossible.

Throughout the morning, Jen went uninspired through the motions of her job: greeting patients, filing papers, answering phones—tears threatening to spill over at any moment. When she couldn't hold them in anymore, a slight trickle swiftly became a torrent. Pent-up emotion erupted. She hurried to the back room, out of sight.

Sandy saw the expression on Jen's face as she brushed past. Her co-worker followed her to the back office.

"Knock, knock," she softly said. "Hey, you okay?" Sandy was probably Jen's closest friend at work. They often took lunch together and chit-chatted during slow times between patients' appointments. She'd felt grateful each time Jennifer opened up about personal issues, which wasn't often. It made those few occasions when she did share feel like small victories.

Jennifer wiped the wetness from her face, hoping to compose herself. No dice. She tried to speak and only cried harder. She settled for shaking her head.

"Can I do anything?"

Jen shook her head again, tears freshly dampening what she'd just brushed off. She still couldn't speak and wouldn't have trusted any words that came out.

"Maybe you should ask to go home?" Sandy offered, kindly.

"Yeah, maybe," Jen finally squeaked out, her voice high, thin, and pained. It was all she could manage.

"Let me know if I can help," Sandy said, giving Jen a gentle smile and pulling the door closed behind her. As usual, Jen hadn't opened up. Sandy wished she could help but knew the best thing she could do was to give her friend privacy.

Left alone, Jennifer fully gave into the tears. She tried to cry quietly but anguished moans escaped as her entire body shook with the agony she felt. She kept asking one word over and over, first in her head and then aloud like a mantra: *Why? Why? Why?*

Unanswered, the question evolved: Why her? Why them? Why now? Why hadn't Marika known this before? Or if she had, why hadn't she told Jen?

Other questions ambushed her. Things she hadn't considered last night pounced: What if Marika did become a man? Did she expect Jennifer to stay? *Could* Jennifer stay? Could she watch her wife transform? Could she be attracted to her as a man? Could she *love* her as a man?

Answers eluded her. The unknown loomed scarier than any bad dream; this was no nightmare figment of the mind. It was real life. Uncertainty threatened to drive her insane. Jen sat on the floor and sobbed.

*****

Spent, Jennifer tried to pull herself together. She dried her tears and went upstairs to find the office manager. They'd never had a great rapport; her boss had a Texas-sized chip on her shoulder that she directed at the younger staff members whenever possible. That included 26-year-old Jen.

Jennifer rapped lightly on the open office door, drawing a breath and squaring her shoulders at the same time. She knew her eyes, red and puffy, would give her away. She couldn't pretend to be sick. Praying her boss wouldn't ask why she needed to leave, she began to speak.

"I have a personal matter that I need to attend to, and—" was all she got out before Lydia interrupted.

Never looking up from her paper-cluttered desk, her boss spoke. "Look, I don't know what's going on, but we're short staffed today, and I can't have you gone too."

Clasping her hands in front of her, unintentionally prayer-like, Jennifer continued. "But I can come in this weekend to make up the—"

"You're gonna need to pull yourself together," Lydia said, firmly, snapping a glance up at her. Under the fluorescent light, she took in Jennifer's tear-swollen eyes before noticing that her still-clasped hands bore no wedding ring. She purposefully put down the document she'd been reviewing, plastered a patronizing smirk on thin lips that might never have tasted a real smile, and continued.

"I know you're young, but let me give you a piece of advice. You should really leave your family life at home." Without formally dismissing her, Lydia turned her attention back to the task at hand as though she'd been interrupted by nothing more than an annoyance—perhaps a noisy cleaning person with a vacuum or a fly buzzing around her head.

Lydia's choice of words hit Jen like a punch in the heart. *Family.* Were they still a family? Would they be if Marika transitioned? What would happen to Jennifer if Marika became a man?

Hurt morphed instantly to red-hot anger. How dare Marika do this! For the first time in her life, Jen had found security. Acceptance. Love without question. Marika accepted her as she was—no expectations and no disappointment. Jen finally felt a sense of self-worth. She knew who she was and where she belonged. But her soulmate was no longer her safe place. She felt abandoned and betrayed, her security as stable as stairs built on quicksand.

Jennifer's world was unraveling by the moment and she was powerless to stop it. Control was an illusion, so was happiness. It was too much.

She slowly walked back to her desk, every step weighing on her as she went. Each thought carried with it alternating waves of sorrow, pain, fury, and despair. The afternoon dragged on.

Jen tried to push through, as her boss had advised. Pull herself together. Leave her family life at home. Put her needs on the back burner so others could take precedence: the office's needs, Lydia's needs, Marika's needs. It was a theme that had repeated itself all her life: putting others first. Always.

*****

Jennifer wrote to pass some of the time, hoping it would help her work through the situation. Poetry had always come easily to her, and she used it now to try to sort her feelings out. These poems would become a coping mechanism for her in the dark days ahead, a way to express in writing what she couldn't verbalize. The pen became her voice: paper, her confessional.

Her poem, *You Got Me ... You Lost,* hints at the crushing blow her self-esteem took at Marika's announcement.

*****

You Got Me ... You Lost

By Jennifer Wyndham

This life is not the one I chose, and not the one I want.
I was chosen to face and overcome these difficult times,
But you got the wrong girl.
You didn't choose one that is strong enough.
You didn't choose the girl who would triumph and be a better person for it.
You got me, and my weakness, and my tears, and my pain.
You got a girl who can't take any more.
You got a girl who wants out.
You got a quitter, a loser.
You didn't get the great human-interest story; triumph over adversity.
You picked me, but you were wrong.
You missed all the girls with strength and confidence and self-worth.
You missed all the girls who want to live life to its fullest, and achieve happiness.

You got me.
You got me, who dwells on the problems, who looks to the past for answers.
You got me, who can't stand up for herself.
You got me, and you lost.

*****

Jennifer would come to feel that Marika was not the only one who lost.
Jen would lose her way, her sense of self, and, very nearly, her life.

Chapter 3
That Girl

She looked like an angel. Porcelain skin, shiny hair that looked like it had been spun of gold. Luminous blue-green eyes filled with hope, reflecting love. As a small child, Jennifer's mother sewed sweet little dresses for her, pairing them with white tights and black patent shoes as though she were a real-life doll. After all, Jen was the second child but the first girl, and her mother took full advantage of any opportunity to adorn her as such.

She adored music and showed a natural rhythm, entertaining her parents as she danced in her playpen to the music of Donna Summer. Her early inclination to dance led to her starting lessons at just three years old. Jennifer took to it immediately, whirling and spinning around the floor. Miniature tutus held an almost princess-like allure to the tot, who reveled in their stiff resistance and loved pushing them down and feeling them spring back into place.

Tiny tap shoes soon lined up next to her little ballet flats. Jennifer would pound out complicated rhythms with her small feet, loving the syncopated sounds she could make.

Years passed and still Jennifer spent hours in the dance studio each week. Stretching. Spinning. Growing. The more difficult the dance, the harder she'd work. Mistakes were not tolerated in Jennifer's young mind and when she messed up, she'd start again, bent on perfection and accepting nothing less. No teacher could have demanded more than Jennifer expected of herself and she constantly strove to be better, sharper, more precise.

Jen idolized the older girls who looked like real-life versions of the ballerina who twirled daintily in her jewelry box. Slim and lithe, they were the epitome of beauty and grace and everything Jennifer wanted to be but feared she never would.

Jazz classes were next, Jen stretching her talents and her muscles with each new routine. She shone in performance, gradually growing into one of the older girls she'd long looked up to.

Dressing rooms were chaotic, a flurry of nerves and false eyelashes. Clouds of hairspray and talcum powder created a haze on the mirror where dozens of dancers fussed and preened, prepping for their next number. In the midst of it all was Jennifer, secretly comparing herself to the others. She was too tall. Too gangly. Too heavy. If only she had a flatter stomach or smaller arms. Years of dance set the stage for the body-image issues that would shadow her life like an unwanted ex-lover who pops up unexpectedly at the worst times.

Jen didn't feel the need to fill her life with boyfriends and stuffed animals and love notes. Dance was enough. Hours and hours of it every week, punishing herself in the studio. Ballet, pointe, tap. Her body flourished on the dance floor, feeling the music, telling a story in a series of carefully choreographed movements.

Jennifer was in her element when she danced. In control, her body responded to every movement and nuance she demanded of herself. It was simultaneously liberating and enslaving, this form of expression that freed her mind while pushing her body almost beyond its limits.

Dance left little room for anything else. When she wasn't in class, she was practicing. She often helped the younger girls with their footwork and arm positions. Reliable and respectful, she was a teacher's dream and the idol of many young dancers.

But dance was more than her passion; it provided an escape from the pressures of middle school, which was especially challenging. There were only five girls in her small private-school class: two sets of best friends, and Jennifer. They shunned the quiet young woman who wanted more than anything to fit in.

"Hey, Four Eyes!" they'd say, paired up in the classroom the same way they paired up anywhere else: four against one. Against her.

"But you all wear glasses too!" she'd counter, not understanding. They'd laugh—cynical, condescending, and oh-so hurtful. "Yeah, but yours are knockoffs. They're not Lacoste."

Her glasses provided only one target. Jennifer's voice, speech, clothing and just about anything else gave them more fodder for taunts. If she mispronounced a word or answered a question incorrectly in class, the jabs were quick and punishing. Jennifer's schoolmates never missed an opportunity to remind her of her place—which was, first and foremost, beneath them.

"You talk funny."

"Did your mom make your clothes? I bet you got that shirt from a second-hand store."

The insults continued, chipping away at any sense of self-esteem Jennifer possessed. She was only sure of herself on the dance floor, coaxing her body to meet her demands—perfection on pointe.

*****

Going out with boys just didn't hold the same allure for Jen as for others her age, so she kept to herself much of the time.

"You have to give people a chance," teachers said.

"You'll find a nice boy when the time is right," her mother said.

Jen tried half-heartedly without much success. The closest she came in middle school was having a boyfriend with whom she held hands—for which she was promptly teased because it was middle school and that was "just babyish." She went to school dances with boys but it never went any further than that. No one really sparked her interest.

In high school, she had a good friend who seemed to hold the potential to be more. He was a bit of a loner too, and they both found solace in their sympathy for each other. But he just disappeared after a few months. No explanation, no breakup. Puzzled and hurt, Jennifer not only found herself without romance, but she'd lost a friend too. Love just didn't seem to be in the cards for her and she was okay with that.

She was distant from Joe, her older brother and only sibling. Both competitive to the core, they tried to one up each other every chance they got. Joe was a good student, and teachers expected Jennifer to follow suit, setting the stage for sibling rivalry from an early age. Her parents expected things of her too: good grades, good behavior, and good dance performances. Jennifer consistently felt the pressure to measure up—and consistently felt she'd missed the mark.

The constant thoughts that she'd let others down weighed on her. Leaving her private school behind, Jennifer excelled grade-wise in public high school but still struggled to feel like she fit in. College proved much the same. She enjoyed a small group of friends but never engaged in the rowdy party scene that defined so many students' college years. Graduating with her communication arts degree from Salisbury University, Jen felt relief to be done with school altogether. Perhaps the world would be more welcoming. She could only try harder for the acceptance that forever seemed to elude her. It was a lonely way to live.

*****

It wasn't until after she finished college that Jen's eyes opened. Her circle of friends widened thanks to work, and she began hanging out with all kinds of people: straight, gay, and lesbian. These friends knew no boundaries when it came to sexuality, and Jennifer watched with deepening interest as all interacted with each other. Suddenly there was no restriction that a date had to be a guy, and 50% of the population that had been off-limits before became an option. Jen met people who were happy and who accepted themselves and gradually realized she hadn't been happy because she hadn't been honest with herself. She didn't date guys because she wasn't into them. Jennifer was a lesbian.

*****

She told Maggie first. An instant message conversation allowed Jennifer to share her news with her friend but still maintain a bit of space between them. Her heart pounding, Jennifer sat with her fingers poised above the keyboard.

"I think I might be gay." Seeing it there on the screen in front of her, it looked so unassuming, not at all hinting at the monumental message it carried. More than five little words strung together; this was her identity and for the first time in her 24 years, she felt like she owned that.

Taking a breath, she hit the "send" button. It was out there. *She* was out.

*****

Some people are simply wired to worry most about making others happy. Jen was one of them. As she waited for Maggie to respond, Jennifer thought back to the times she'd shopped with her mom. Having fought her weight most of her life, Cindy hated trying on clothes herself, but she'd encourage Jennifer to try on the outfits she wished she could wear. The clothes weren't Jen's style, but she'd dutifully put them on, coming brightly out of the dressing room as though they were the most beautiful thing she'd ever seen.

"What do you think?" she'd ask, twirling so Cindy could get a 360-degree view. "Oh, honey," her mom would say. "I love it! Let's get it!"

And they would. Jennifer could've left the clothes in her closet, but she'd wear them anyway—outfits that weren't at all her style—simply because it made her mother happy. That was Jen: always the peacemaker. This self-discovery, the realization that she was gay, went against the grain. It was not going to make everyone happy, and Jen knew it.

*****

It didn't take long for Maggie (who was also gay) to show up at Jen's apartment with her girlfriend in tow to talk about it.

"Are you sure?"

"How long have you known?"

"What do you think your parents will say?"

"Is there someone you wanna ask out?"

Jen fielded the questions as best she could. Yes, she was sure. She hadn't known long. Her parents would be devastated. And no, there was no one in particular.

Maggie was persistent. Speaking from experience, she tried to warn her about what to expect next. "You know this is not going to be easy, right? I mean, God, when I came out I was a wreck. Especially when I told my parents! My dad didn't talk to me for weeks!"

Jen was well aware that this news was not going to sit well with her folks. "I know. I'm already dreading telling my mom."

"You don't have to tell her right away, you know. But I'm so glad you told me! How are you feeling now that it's out there?"

"Better. Good. Excited, actually! But it still feels sorta ... unreal."

More questions and answers volleyed back and forth for hours like a tennis match until Jennifer had convinced them (and maybe to a small degree, herself) that this was real. It was a long, dramatic discussion that left her spent and a bit dazed, but also relieved. She was one giant step closer to self-acceptance.

Not long after that, she met Marika, who'd only recently moved to the Eastern Shore, home of world-class seafood and wild pony swims. The two met online after Marika created a website profile to meet other gay people in the area. Jennifer's profile popped up and Marika sent an instant message. Jen's "away" message popped up, letting Marika know she wasn't online.

"Your mom," the away message said.

Marika laughed aloud at the randomness of the response, certain she wanted to become friends with this woman simply based on her sense of humor.

*****

Marika's invitation to connect awaited the unknowing Jen, who'd just finished running errands. Dropping the mail on the table (bills and more bills—just whose great idea was it to become a grownup?), she sat at the desk and logged on. The computer screen turned gray, then white, loading a dating website laden with pictures and profiles. The small icon in the corner alerted her that she had a message waiting. She couldn't have possibly known as she clicked it that the woman who sent it would change her life.

*****

Internet dating sites were in their infancy at that point. Jennifer and Marika chatted online plenty over those first few days, each looking forward to hearing the familiar "ding" sound that would let them know the other was online. Their Internet chats covered the basics.

"Where do u work?" Marika typed.

"I teach dance," came Jen's reply. The words appeared on the screen one letter at a time as Jen typed them.

Marika couldn't resist. "What kind of dance? Exotic? Haha."

Jennifer responded with a winky face emoticon. "Ballet and tap. Nothing unusual. What about u?"

"I'm on WLAF." Marika was proud of her job and smiled as she typed it, even though Jen couldn't see her grin.

"Wow, cool," came Jen's response.

"Ever listen?"

"I will now."

"I'm the one with the sexy voice. Lol."

Indeed, she was. Jen tuned in and something about Marika's voice touched her in a way she hadn't felt before. Jen started calling in and the two women would talk during songs, discussing everything from likes and dislikes to politics, food choices, and anything in between. Conversation between them flowed easily via phones and keyboards, and they learned they both enjoyed music and possessed a similar sarcasm that made the other laugh. It wasn't long before they exchanged pictures and made plans to meet in person.

*****

Marika had to work the night they met, so it was 11:30 before they could catch up with each other at Maggie's apartment. Marika pulled into the parking lot and was immediately taken with Jennifer's statuesque appearance as she stood waiting outside. Her stance and 5'8" physique stunned the 5'1" Marika, who became nervous and hyper. At first it overwhelmed the reserved Jennifer.

God, she's kind of a spaz! Jen thought.

But it didn't take long for Marika to settle down once they started talking.

"You're taller than I expected."

"I hope that's not a bad thing," Jen said, apprehensively, but she was pretty sure Marika hadn't meant it negatively.

"Not at all. When you're short you get used to everyone being taller." Nervous laughter.

"It's nice to have a face to go with the voice I've been hearing. But I have to admit, I'm not a huge fan of the music you guys play."

"But you listen anyway?"

"Ummm... actually, I listen when you're talking, and then I turn it down when the songs start," Jen admitted, feeling a little guilty. She didn't want to hurt Marika's feelings.

"That's awesome!" Marika beamed.

They chatted for a long time, lounging against the car. Eventually, they headed inside and sat facing each other on the couch, sharing thoughts, dreams, hopes, fears. Before they knew it, it was 4:00 am. The two women headed outside to say goodbye.

Under the glow of the street lamp, Marika saw a pen gleaming on the floor of the car. She came up with a plan.

"I bet you have great handwriting."

"How do you know?" Jen asked, perplexed.

"Here, I'll prove it." She retrieved the pen and handed it to Jennifer. "Take this pen and write your name here."

Marika held out her palm, her breath catching slightly as Jennifer took her hand to write her name. It was their first opportunity to touch. Jen's soft skin felt warm on Marika's and both felt an undeniable tingle at the touch.

"Knew it," Marika said softly. She wasn't referring to the handwriting, and they both knew it.

With sunrise approaching and a workday ahead for Jennifer, the women reluctantly parted ways but made plans for a proper date that weekend. While it wasn't love at first sight, it made Jennifer feel things she hadn't experienced before. For the first time, she was hopeful.

*****

"Don't pick me up. My parents are home," Jennifer said.

"It's okay. I don't mind. I'll put on a good show," Marika joked.

Marika arrived to what she could only describe as a "Leave it to Beaver" house. Freshly baked apple pie sat tantalizingly on the counter, the aroma filling the tidy living room.

Oh God, she thought. *If this is how Jen grew up, this just might not work out*, she worried, quickly flashing to thoughts of her bipolar mother and the emotional chaos that marked her childhood.

Jen put her fears to rest though, explaining her mom had been on a cleaning spree that day. "I swear, it's not normally like this," she asserted, assuring Marika there was no reason to be intimidated. The two got out of there quickly, though, as anxious to start their date as they were to escape the Cleaver-esque atmosphere at the house.

They dined outside at a gastro pub in Salisbury, where the smell of seafood teased their nostrils as they waited for dinner to arrive. Both were nervous but enjoying the time together.

"I'll have the scallops," Jen told the waitress, who hovered too much. The couple kept laughing about how frequently she interrupted them to ask if they wanted more bread.

"Chicken Chesapeake for me, please," Marika said. "And no more bread, thanks," which made Jennifer laugh.

They joked as though they'd known each other forever—each feeling that somehow, they had.

A stroll around the nearby plaza after dinner meant more conversation and both felt relaxed as they opened up to each other, enjoying the feeling that the date was going well.

And it continued long past the meal. The pair went over to Maggie's apartment and watched movies, sitting close to each other and not-so accidentally brushing hands. Their first kiss was electric—right before it was interrupted by the arrival of more friends who'd come to hang out. It was a date that lasted the night, with Jennifer and Marika falling asleep in each other's arms on the couch. Both knew they'd found someone special.

Before either one of them knew it, they were talking about the future. They moved in to their two-bedroom apartment and began their life together. Even still, Jen couldn't bring herself to tell her parents about her lifestyle or her relationship. With two bedrooms in the apartment, she let them believe she and Marika were just roommates. Expectations die hard, and she was reluctant to kill those of her parents'.

*****

The day finally came when she was ready. She and Marika been dating for a year and living together for about six months. Jen knew they were going to get engaged, and she had to tell her parents that not only was she in love, but in love with a woman.

There was the usual small talk as they sat in her mom's kitchen. Cindy, Jennifer's mom, filled her in on the latest news from her world. Jen tried to quell her nerves long enough to seem interested, but only heard pieces of what her mom was saying.

"… and the new minister at church seems to be fitting right in. I really like his sermons," Cindy said.

Jen took a sip of water and steeled herself, mentally rehearsing her announcement while her mom jumped from one topic to another.

Cindy placed a dish filled with guacamole on the table in front of Jennifer. "Dad loved it, and I think you'll like it too. But I want to make it without the cilantro next time to see whether it's better that way. Maybe—

"Yeah, I'd like the recipe." Jennifer braced herself for her mother's reaction. "Uh, Mom, Marika and I … well, I don't know quite how to tell you this, but … we're dating. She is not just my roommate. I'm in love with her."

The silence was deafening, the sound of years of her parents' expectations and dreams dying in a horrific explosion before falling unrealized to the ground.

"I'm … glad you told me. I didn't expect this from you, but I love you," Cindy spoke a bit falteringly.

"Thanks, Mom. I'm really glad you know. Thanks for understanding." Cindy didn't seem to have much more to say, and Jennifer, relieved, took advantage of the chance to redirect the conversation, which became very superficial. Neither of them addressed anything of any substance for the remainder of the visit—which was their pattern when either was upset. "Keep it light," seemed to be an unspoken agreement between them.

The visit finally over, Jen headed home. Could it really be that easy? Jennifer, who'd waited until her twenties before realizing she was gay, could share the news with her mother and be accepted for it just like that? Turns out, it was more complicated than that. The phone rang at Jennifer and Marika's apartment later that evening.

"She's brainwashing you. This isn't you!" Cindy cried. "Marika is taking advantage of you. You should come home. You can't handle this. She's going to hurt you and then where will you be?"

Jen listened not-so patiently, absorbing her mother's words, letting them swirl around her as the worlds' expectations always had.

"Your glasses look funny!"

"You're Joe's sister—we expect good things from you."

"You'll find a nice boy."

Her heart sank. Not so easy after all. Jen swallowed her words, refusing to argue. She turned to her standard way to close an awkward or difficult conversation.

"Well, that's about it," Jen said. "I guess I'll talk to you later." With a sigh, she told her mother she loved her and gently got off the phone.

And just like that, the cloak of expectations was off. She felt freer than ever, allowed to live her life no longer worried about her parents' reaction. And fortunately, Cindy simply needed time to come to terms with her daughter being a lesbian. It would take less than a month for her to come around to realizing that Jen was still Jen—that she simply preferred to have a relationship with a woman instead of a man. In seemingly no time, Cindy included Marika when she was planning things and began referring to Jennifer and Marika as "You girls."

"Could you girls come over for dinner on Saturday?" Cindy would ask.

Or, "We thought we'd take you girls out for ice cream tonight, if you're free."

Jennifer was thrilled when Cindy mentioned she'd been looking for a local chapter of PFLAG, which used to be known as Parents, Families and Friends of Lesbians and Gays. Her mother's acceptance of her lifestyle, while not immediate, was now unquestionable.

And with her approval, Jennifer had found herself more at peace than she'd ever been. She knew who she was, and she'd found her true love. She was living the perfect life.

She didn't know it was all about to change.

Chapter 4
What's in a Name?

Wake

Heavy like lead,
My head weighs on my pillow.
Muscles ache, they refuse to work.
Mind over body, a battle rages
Bright light through the blinds
Taunts me.
Searing pain in my heart reminds me
This is my life,
This is all there is.

Willing it to go away,
i sink deeper into myself.
Guilt nags at me.
Make it go away!
Leave me be.
Leave me lonely.
i beg for rest;
For release from this chain.
This chain, this existence.
Set me free; let me go…

*****

Two long weeks since the disastrous Valentine's Day. Fourteen days for Jennifer to think about Marika's announcement that she felt like a man. Jen was taking it day by day, going to work and pretending everything was okay. She'd put her wedding ring back on the day after she removed it, but it didn't seem to hold the eternal promise it once had.

Jennifer kept wondering whether this was the end of her marriage. If Marika transitioned, it meant more than a change of gender; it would be a life-altering change for both of them. The decision meant Jennifer's whole vision of her married life would be turned inside out and upside down.

She remembered coming out to her mother, to her friends. That was enough of a life-changing event. Shattering the world's—and her parent's—expectations had been unthinkably stressful for this woman who'd always done what was expected of her. She didn't like to make waves. A people-pleaser, Jennifer had dug deep inside to come to terms with her sexuality, knowing it would be less-than acceptable to the bulk of society and, more importantly, her parents. And now she faced something even more out of the ordinary.

Marika's self-revelation and disclosure demanded a decision of Jennifer that in some ways seemed so very straightforward. Stay or go. Two choices with a non-existent gray area between them. Stay, and accept that she was powerless to stop Marika's progression to become a man. Stay and try to come to grips with the fact that she'd be *married* to a man. Changing Marika's mind wasn't an option for her. If this is what Marika needed to be happy, Jen wouldn't block her. Which meant she either needed to accept the decision and learn to deal with it or walk away from her marriage and leave her soulmate: relinquish the life-long love she'd so recently pledged.

More than a difficult decision, it was a heartbreaking one. And rather than making it, this modern-day Scarlett O'Hara had decided not to think about it. It was simply too much for her brain to handle, so Jennifer decided not to decide. She filed it away, knowing it couldn't stay trapped there forever but holding some sort of unrealistic hope that if she didn't give it credence, it would cease to exist. Jennifer just tried to go about her life as she had before the announcement, plodding along, one foot and then the other.

Days dragged on as they both went through the motions. Eating dinner, doing dishes, washing clothes. Jennifer had picked up a cold in the meantime, laying low and sleeping through the worst of it. The sleep might've been a coping mechanism for her mind and heart as much as it was a way to heal her body, but Jennifer didn't dwell on its intent. Instead, she preferred to enjoy the blissful nothingness that allowed her to escape a reality that threatened to crash down at any moment. When she slept, she didn't think. That was good enough for her.

And then Marika called from work. They hadn't talked much about the movie or the discussion that occurred afterwards—both of them scared to broach the subject and wary of the other's reaction. The phone rang and Jen answered, standing at the kitchen sink, looking out the closed kitchen window that held the promise of an open world. She listened as Marika's voice, which had so recently soothed her with its tones, came through the phone line.

"Hey babe." Nothing about Marika's voice had changed, but it didn't touch Jen the way it used to. The current circumstances made Jennifer feel far more distant from her spouse than the telephone line that separated them.

"Hey yourself. How's it going?" (*Funny how conversations become rote. Respond without thinking*, Jen thought.)

"Good. I'm gonna stop by the grocery store on my way home. Need anything?" Marika offered.

"Yeah, actually. Maybe some chocolate ice cream?"

"You got it." And then, without segueing, "So, I think I'm going to change my name," Marika said.

Inside, Jennifer screamed: pain, anguish and fear fighting for the top spot. Suddenly she felt so very alone. She had been dreading this moment ever since that evening and here it was. *What the fuck? Why are you doing this to me? I love you! I love US, just as we are! And I'm not sure I can handle this!*

After an eternal pause during which she could've run a marathon and finished last, Jen spoke. Her voice was tame, almost controlled—completely unlike the thoughts rebelling in her mind.

"Why do you feel like you need to do that?" she softly questioned. Almost an afterthought, she continued, "What would you change it to?"

"Marc, with a c." The first question went unanswered.

Crushed, Jen sat on that for what seemed like hours. She rolled it around in her mind. Marc. So simple. Unassuming. It suited Marika's personality, the flippant "c" just like her, whimsical. But it wasn't Marika. It was *Marc*. The more she mulled it over, the more absurd it seemed. Pain that began as a dull ache grew until it roared through her, searing her soul. *Marc!* How could those four letters puncture her heart this way?

Jennifer finally summoned up her courage to ask questions she really didn't want answered.

"Well, what?" she demanded. "Are you gonna do hormones?" She nearly spat out the next one: "And start dressing like a man?" And then, nearly hysterically, "How far are you taking this? Where's the stopping point?"

The questions spewed out of her, tumbling one on top of another as her anger and angst mounted inside. It was more than she could take, more than she could even think about. Numbness started creeping up slowly, overtaking the pain that had just coursed through her. Jennifer thought she might pass out.

But Marika, who was still struggling with her new identity, couldn't really provide any clarity. She still wasn't sure where this path was leading; instead, like Jennifer, she was taking it one step at a time. The end wasn't in sight. Rather than a straight line drawn with a Sharpie and a ruler, it was more like a series of dots that would eventually be connected that led her from here to … somewhere else. Some*one* else. Someone who felt like her but looked totally different. Someone who called to her from the inside, begging to be recognized for who he was.

"I don't know," Marika said, simply. And it was the truth. She really, truly didn't know how far this journey would take her. She only knew she needed to start it and let it lead where it may.

It was Jen's first reality check. The signs she'd been dreading for the past two weeks were all but pummeling her. The future she'd begun to fear now loomed as a twisted, misshapen silhouette of an unknown life that looked nothing like she'd planned. Her wife was taking steps to become a man, and she was powerless to stop it.

*****

Marika and Marc

You are as different as:
Night and day
Dark and light
Woman and man

But as alike as:

Two summer days
Two shades of blue
Two beats of my heart

Marika is a light snowfall and a sandy beach
Marc is a blizzard and a lonely desert

Marika is my world as I always imagined it
Marc is my life that is falling to pieces

Marika is in every smile and every laugh
Marc is in every cut and every tear.

*****

Jennifer hung the phone up, pressing the button as hard as she could as though she could take out her frustrations by making the black plastic submit. The phone acquiesced without changing her life or providing the answers she so desperately needed. The damned thing went silent, and Jen turned her attention inward to the decision she'd tried so fiercely to squelch.

Why should anyone have to decide this? she wondered. *Why me? Why now?* Her perfect reality had been in her grasp. She'd been the good girl, she'd done what was asked of her and thought she'd been rewarded by finding her soulmate. Why was that being ripped away from her?

Questions swirled around her like a tempest, making her brain fuzzy and her head throb. Fingers of doubt, anger, and resentment swirled in amongst the questions, filling the tempest with black, grey, and white so that it became a muted tornado of color that twisted inside her like a hurricane of hurt. She nearly crawled to the bed, determined to find the peace that only sleep could provide.

*****

(Untitled)

i see in black and white
there is color out there,
but i don't see it.
someone turned my colors off.

roses are red, violets are blue
it's all black and white to me.
the angry red is gone;

green jealousy has faded away.
no calm blue; no quiet green.
it's all black and white for me.

black for the darkness in my heart.
white; blank like my mind.
the yellow sun doesn't shine for me anymore,
violets don't bloom.
my rainbow is held hostage.
it's all black and white in me.

Chapter 5
Marika

Marika had always felt different. She knew she was not like everyone else but she didn't know why. Maybe everyone else felt they were different too. Maybe the whole world just pretended to feel normal, and that is what normal was: pretending to be something you weren't. Or maybe it had to do with her childhood—a mosaic of memories held together by the thinnest strip of normalcy.

Marika didn't know when the trouble between her parents started; it seemed it had always been there. Living together but disconnected in their small military housing unit was status quo. It was common to walk past the family room and see Dad zoned out in front of the TV, cracking open yet another can of Coors with each commercial break. To Marika, that sound became as recognizable as the start of an episode of Barney.

Born in Japan, Marika was a Navy brat. Her family endured the usual short stints in different locations. When she was six, her father abruptly moved out. There was no preparation for it; one day, her parents had a knock-down, drag-out argument and the next, Dad was gone.

She was too young to know the word "bipolar," and many healthcare professionals hadn't yet gotten too familiar with it either. After all, this was the early 80s, and the diagnosis of manic depression hadn't yet become as prevalent as it is today. Even if she knew the word, Marika wouldn't have understood that it was the reason her mother was so irrational. She simply knew she needed to try really hard not to upset her mom.

She'd tried to make herself smaller. If she were invisible, maybe her mother would forget about her. She tiptoed through the house pretending to be just that—invisible—until her mom would notice her and fly off the handle.

Her one constant ally in life? Her brother, Edward. Six years older and fathered by a different man, Edward helped his sister as best he could. Unfortunately, he was no match for their mother, who could turn from sweet to unpredictably sour in no time flat.

Marika's father moving out didn't tame her mother's frenetic episodes. She simply developed other triggers that sent her into a tailspin. Marika remembered her mom dating one guy in particular. After they broke up, her mom pulled out every stitch of the guy's clothing and ordered Edward and Marika to cut it all up and throw it out on the porch. Scared to disobey, the two kids dutifully did as they were told, slicing and cutting the fabric as though it were a school project. She watched as strips of cloth fluttered to the ground outside like confetti at a parade. It was fun for Marika (what a wild thing to be given permission to do!) but years later, she recognized it as indicative of depths of her mother's instability.

Life continued on an uneven keel for Marika. She never knew when the next outburst would come, and she lived in fear of the unknown. Her mother would storm into her room without warning, trashing everything in sight and demanding Marika clean it up. She never knew what she'd done wrong, but she understood the urgency with which she needed to straighten it up afterwards. It was an unsettling and unhappy way to grow up.

Due to their recurrent relocations, Marika wasn't granted the comfort of a friend or a favorite teacher to confide in. Soon after the divorce, her mother started a serious relationship with another Navy man, one who was good to Marika and her brother. Between moving because of his military status and Marika going to live with her father for short stints of time, she was on the move too much to make any lasting relationships. In fourth grade alone she attended four schools in two states. Making friends wasn't worth the inevitable goodbyes.

Besides, there was that nagging feeling that there was something wrong with her. Certainly, her mom's episodes didn't help, like the time her brother took Marika with him to a friends' house. They came home to a locked door. Edward didn't have his key.

"Mom! Can you unlock the door?"

"Forget it. You wanna go out? Hang out with your friends? Then you just stay out!"

"Come on, Mom! We just went over to Steve's house. Marika's hungry. Let us in!"

"Maybe next time you'll come home when you're supposed to."

Edward and Marika stayed outside, huddled and whispering together for hours—all because they'd been gone too long in their mother's mind.

"We should've come back sooner," Marika whimpered. She sat with her knees against her chest, her long shirt down pulled over top of her legs like a tent, wrapping her arms around herself to try to warm up. She was cold and scared. As difficult as her mother's moods could be, her mom was one of only two constant presences in her life, and now she'd gone and done something to upset her. Again. What if Mom decided she wasn't worth sticking around for? What if she left too?

By middle school, Marika accepted the fact that home was never going to be her "normal" place. She turned her attention to school instead, stretching her wings and letting more of her goofy personality show. And it worked—she made friends.

One particular day, Marika and a small group had gathered in a classroom to hang out after lunch. There was the usual talk of who had a crush on whom, or what the math teacher had assigned for homework.

"I heard Katie kissed Matthew Swenson!" Eileen said.

Erica, who never went without a piece of gum in her mouth, blew and popped a giant bubble before responding. "Ewww. He's so gross. Jacob said he doesn't brush his teeth. He stinks." She jammed another piece of pink Bubbalicious in her mouth and smacked away.

The clock marked the seconds off with a loud *click* each time the secondhand moved. They had 10 more minutes before class. Most of the girls were flipping through glossy-paged volumes of *Young Miss* magazine, checking out the latest in everything beauty-related. Images of perfectly adorned young ladies graced the pages, each exuding a bold confidence that, in reality, had eluded every middle school girl since the beginning of time.

"Ooh, this one's cute! Look at how they did the back!" Corrinne gushed.

"God, I wish I had curls like that. Mom won't let me get a perm until I'm fifteen." Jane was always lamenting her stick-straight hair that refused to hold a curl from the curling iron she used steadfastly each morning.

Her friends had often tried to get Marika to change her hairstyle. She wore her hair long and straight. The group hounded her frequently, urging her to try the latest in French braids or a tousled 'do.

Anna, a pretty girl (with stylish hair, naturally), was brushing Marika's brown locks, intent that today would be the day she finally convinced her friend to wear layers like Rachel on *Friends*. "You should at least try it. It's so cute. All the girls are wearing their hair like that."

As though a light switch had been flipped, Marika grabbed the brush from Anna and flung it across the room. "I'm not a girl!" she cried out. It was the first time she'd said the words, and they left her mouth without any forethought. The outburst as unpredictable and unexplainable as any of her mother's, and she brushed it off almost as soon as it happened. It would be years before she even thought about it again.

Interestingly, her clothing choices underscored that sentiment and always had. She'd resisted dresses for as long as she could remember, crying when her mother insisted she wear a dress when it was time to go meet the ships coming in. Marika much preferred jeans with baggy shirts—especially after she noticed her breasts starting to develop. She wore sports bras and was grateful for her small cup size that was easily disguised. While other girls might've used socks or tissues to appear more developed, Marika was happy to hide any outward sign of femininity under a loose top.

And the other sign of womanhood? She'd been through sex ed, and she knew what to expect when the time came. Still, she hoped and prayed that by some miracle she just would never get a period. Most girls look forward to that event as a sign of their impending maturity; Marika found just the thought of it disgusting and unnatural. When her cycle started in her freshman year of high school, she cried at the utter unfairness of it all. Being a female was, in her pubescent mind, *gross*.

Ironically, ninth grade was also the same year she had to start changing clothes for gym. Girls around her chatted as they stripped down and suited up, casually walking naked to and from the shower without a second thought. Marika did everything she could not to show her body, carefully layering her clothes and removing them in a cumbersome disrobing ritual that showed as little skin as possible. It was clunky and uncomfortable, much like every other part of her adolescence.

*****

High school also meant dating. Marika was as outgoing as she was socially awkward, and her gregariousness attracted attention. She had a handful of boyfriends but nothing serious. It wasn't until her senior year that she was pretty certain she was a lesbian. *"Maybe that's why I never feel normal,"* she thought to herself. She was dating Ron at the time, and she'd lost her virginity to him. It had been a forgettable experience that left her even less interested in boys. She came up with a plan and laid it out to him.

"You ever thought about being with two girls? I'd be okay with that, if you wanted to have another girl with us."

"No way," he said, and he meant it. He was happy with the way things were. Marika, on the other hand, was not. She'd thought that a threesome would give her a chance to experience sex with another woman, to be sure that what she suspected was true. Ron's dismissal of the idea was his undoing. Marika broke off the relationship. Deep down, she didn't really need to have a threesome with him to confirm her sexuality.

She came out to her best friend first, who was supportive and, perhaps coincidentally, also a lesbian. (Even more coincidental, that same best friend would later be the one who introduced her to the concept of being gender queer, when she herself transitioned to become a man.) Marika felt like she'd finally figured out how to fit in and be comfortable with people, and the thought of a whole new world opening to her was exhilarating. She dated girls off and on for the next few years without a serious relationship.

But high school was about more than dating. Marika played in the school band and enjoyed being known as a band geek. She did *not* enjoy the uniforms they had to wear for concerts, however. The guys wore tuxedos; the girls, long black polyester dresses. Marika had a panic attack the first time she put one on. She requested to be allowed to wear a tuxedo and was turned down. As they had from the time she was little, dresses continued to irritate her.

And then of course, there was prom. Marika asked a female friend to go with her and while the two weren't dating, they were looking forward to a fun night. When a classmate saw them and expressed disgust at two women together, she had the last laugh. "My date's hotter than your date," she retorted. He shut up.

*****

At seventeen, Marika came out to her mother. There was no drama: no big buildup. Sitting in the kitchen, the two were drinking coffee. Marika looked up from her mug, caught her mother's eye, and said the words bluntly, "I'm gay." Equally bluntly, her mom told her she already knew. It was anticlimactic but also a relief. She felt better having shared the information. She didn't like secrets.

Having heard horror stories from others, she knew just how fortunate she was not to have had any horrible experiences with coming out. Being open about who she was helped Marika feel less different. She still had a sense that something wasn't as it should be, but maybe as she told more people that feeling would dissipate.

*****

"Hey, can you grab that?" Marika was lounging on Stephanie's couch when the doorbell rang. She'd been spending a lot of time at Steph's since high school graduation. With no job and no classes to go to, there wasn't much else to do.

Stephanie had gone into the kitchen to grab some Cokes from the fridge.

The bell rang again and Marika pulled herself away from the video game long enough to open the door.

A Marine recruiter stood in front of her, there to talk with Steph's brother. Marika called up to Alex and told him he had company. The two men went into the kitchen to talk while Stephanie and Marika finished their game. Before leaving, the recruiter struck up a conversation with the women. His timing couldn't have been better.

Marika was really unsure about her future. She didn't like the idea of traditional college. She told the recruiter she'd be interested in joining the Marines but only if she could play trombone in the Marine Corps band. The next thing she knew, Marika had passed the ASVAB test and had signed on the dotted line. It was only then they told her there were no trombone openings in the band. As a backup plan, she requested a position in legal administration, signals intelligence, or military police. She was not selected for any of them. Instead, she was going to serve her country as a Marine admin. She was disappointed in the position but not in her decision to serve as a Marine. That branch above all others appealed to her because it was hardcore and would give her a chance to prove herself.

Marika committed to four years of service. The commitment didn't scare her, the military's stance on homosexuality did. She read the rules of conduct with a growing dread, reviewing the list of things that could get her kicked out. This was going to be a challenge. She thought that if she just didn't say she was gay, maybe they wouldn't figure it out.

*****

Boot camp was, in a word, fun. At least for Marika. It was where she learned to swim. She found that she enjoyed the structure and routine of camp, and she thrived on testing herself physically. And she found the drill instructors' antics riotously funny. Her brother Edward (also in the Marines) had warned Marika about the mind games the drill instructors play. Thanks to her mother's wild manic-depressive episodes, she was more than prepared. The angrier the instructors got, the funnier Marika found the whole situation. They couldn't break her. She wasn't the most fit, and she certainly wasn't physically the strongest, but she was well-trained for the mental barrage that defines boot camp. And she loved that even during the times when she was one of the weaker recruits, her fellow Marines cheered her on. It felt like family.

Like all women in the Marines, Marika attended boot camp in Parris Island, South Carolina. She successfully completed the thirteen-week stint, learning everything from hand-to-hand combat skills and sharp shooting to warrior training.

After graduation, she was assigned to Jacksonville, North Carolina, where she tried once again to be invisible. It wasn't that she didn't like the people—far from it. She loved the feeling of belonging. She loved the

camaraderie. At the same time, she was desperately afraid someone would discover her sexuality. The hardcore pressure to keep it hidden was rough. When male Marines would hit on her, she tried hard to crack a joke and escape with no one the wiser.

"Hey, Crawford!" (All Marines were called by their last name.) "Want to go catch the new Tom Cruise movie with me?"

"Nah, thanks. I'm not a fan. He's not tall enough." She walked her 5'1" self away quickly.

Or, "There's a dart tournament Friday. Be my partner? I'll buy ya a beer."

"Sorry, already got plans," Marika would answer. "My friend is coming, and I'm going to show her around town." (Marika *did* have a friend coming to town. Her girlfriend of several months would be visiting.) "Hope you win!"

She felt a mounting pressure regarding her sexual preference and her ability to keep it secret. Of course, it didn't take long for her to discover she wasn't alone. Within a handful of months, she'd learned of other gays on her base. A group of them headed out on the weekends to Wilmington or some other bigger city nearby, visiting gay clubs. It felt good to be herself again. It also gave her a false sense of security.

It was only a matter of time before Marika was caught.

Despite the military's "Don't ask, don't tell" policy, three people were discharged for homosexuality and an active search was underway by base authorities to identify anyone who was gay. Marika heard the scuttlebutt, and a close friend told her that her own name had been raised as a possible target. She faced a choice. She could wait and see if they caught her and be dishonorably discharged, or she could confess and be honorably discharged. She opted for the truth. After just ten months, Marika's military career was over.

*****

Marika dated sporadically. She had a long-distance, short-lived relationship with the woman who visited her during her time in the Marines. They actually lived together for a brief time but it didn't last. Marika also had a two-plus year romance that prompted her to give her girlfriend a ring, a wonderfully romantic gesture that held bright promise. Right up until they broke up because her girlfriend decided she was straight, after all.

From her mother's bipolar episodes when she was younger to the recently broken engagement, Marika's first two decades had proven to be a rollercoaster of emotions. Little did she know she would soon embark on a ride wilder than anything she'd experienced so far.

Chapter 6

The Day My Wife Became My Husband

Marika held the name-change form in front of her. She was about to go from being Marika Sharon Crawford to Marc Marika Wyndham. (She had decided to drop her real father's last name in favor of her stepdad's, who'd raised her.) Filling out the form, it was strange to see *Marc*, but at the same time it felt right—like a familiar friend you've only just met. Marika couldn't wait to tell others, and one of the first was her boss.

There are plenty of jobs out there where making a transition wouldn't affect daily work; Marika's wasn't one of them. As a radio personality, her voice filled the local airwaves every day. Testosterone would change her voice, and no one knew just what it would sound like once the transition was complete, which meant she'd have to be off air for a while. She asked for a private meeting with the radio station's general manager.

"So, you know I'm always one for surprises," Marika started the conversation. She liked her boss and was both excited to share her news and hopeful he'd take it well.

"Don't tell me," her boss said, holding up his hand as though he could physically stop news he didn't want to hear.

"I'm not leaving."

"Okay, then tell me." He listened as Marika explained what she was about to do, and he was supportive of the change. They agreed that Marika could work behind the scenes during the transition to allow her voice time to change.

Telling her co-workers went smoothly, all things considered. They all assembled in the station's conference room, unsure of why they were being called together. Marika spoke first to the group gathered around the table.

"I'm sure you're wondering why I've called you all here," she joked to break the ice. There was nervous laughter, mostly emanating from Marika herself. She often turned to humor as a defense mechanism; this time was no different. She forged ahead.

"I've decided to transition to become a man, and I'd like for you all to start calling me Marc," she said. "Please also use male pronouns when you're talking about me." The words tumbled out quickly. She hadn't gotten comfortable with telling people just yet, and her spiel was as rushed as it was earnest.

There was silence following her announcement, but it was a respectful quiet.

"When I start hormones, my voice is gonna change like I'm a 13-year-old going through puberty!" Laughter, but this time from everyone in the room. She continued, "Rather than embarrass the hell out of myself and the station by sounding like Peter Brady on the air, we figure it makes sense for me to be behind the scenes for a while until my voice settles down."

If anyone had an issue with her decision, they kept silent. Her coworkers congratulated her, applauded her courage, and went back to work. Some of them may have whispered about it behind her back, but on the surface, anyway, they were supportive.

For Marika, it was an easy part of the transition. For Jennifer, it was another matter.

*****

"Don't I get a say in whether we tell people?" she asked after they'd gone out with friends one evening. They were back at the house, cleaning up before bed. Jen was putting the last of the dishes away from the dishwasher while Marika filled it with the dirty dishes from the sink. The teamwork felt comfortable, the conversation did not.

Each time Marika told someone, it felt like a dagger in Jen's heart. "It's like you're telling everyone we see." Jen found it embarrassing and self-indulgent. "Like my life is 'The Marc Show,' and it's all about you. I'm standing in the wings, watching my own life happen without me."

Her resentment grew.

*****

Others caught on pretty quickly to using Marika's new name-to-be, Marc. Jennifer resisted. Whether it was out of spite, denial, or resentment (or maybe all three), she took her time using her wife's new name. Instead, she used "Mar" for months, which had been an occasional nickname before and now seemed a suitable way to bridge the two names. It felt androgynous, without any gender, and it gave her time to adapt while still trying to honor Marika's needs.

"Did you find your keys, Mar?"

"Hey, Mar, it's your turn to feed the cat."

"Mar, can you grab the phone?"

It was about this time that Jennifer started seeing a therapist. The idea sprang from Marika's therapy sessions, which Jennifer would occasionally attend as a way to better understand this process that so confused her. Ultimately, she decided maybe personal therapy sessions would help her cope.

"Tell me why you find it so difficult," Jackie, her therapist, prodded in her session one day. "Why is it hard to say 'Marc?'"

"I'm not sure," Jen said. "I guess 'cause I still don't want it to be real. And maybe that makes it real. Like maybe if I don't say it, it's not gonna happen?" Meant to be a statement, her thought ended with a question mark. *Wishful thinking*, Jen figured.

This was Jackie's second appointment with Jennifer, and it was easy to see how lost Jen felt within her own life. Jackie'd encouraged Jennifer to take her time getting comfortable with the name change and the myriad adjustments her marriage was undergoing.

"Tell me about Marc's plans," she urged, intentionally using the new name in hopes of getting Jen used to it.

"She's ... he's ..." Jen corrected herself. "*Mar* has already told the station manager about the transition."

"Do you think he will take the next step and start hormones?" Jackie watched as Jen spun her wedding ring in endless circles around her finger. The fading afternoon light far shone brighter than Jen's mood. It was easy to see the toll the changes were taking on her patient. Dark circles under her eyes, Jen clearly wasn't sleeping well.

Jen sighed, tears forming before her next words had. "Yeah, that's the plan," she responded, her misery evident.

"And how do you feel about that?"

"Lousy." Jen's tears flowed.

"Why?" Jackie handed her a tissue, watching her patient's face contort with pain as she struggled to answer.

"Because I like things the way they were! I was happy!"

"And you don't think you can be happy with Marc?"

It was the first time anyone had asked her point blank, and it caught Jennifer off guard. *It's still Marika in there*, she thought. *No matter what she calls herself, she's still the woman I fell in love with.* She took a moment, wiping at the salty tears that seemed a constant companion these days.

"Maybe I can. I don't know," she admitted. "And I'm scared to find out."

"You don't have to decide anything right now," Jackie reminded her. "And you shouldn't expect to have all the answers." She'd noticed Jennifer's comfort with structure. Predictability was obviously important to her young patient. "Just because it's different doesn't mean you won't like it. Give yourself time to get used to the idea. And maybe, just here with me, try using 'Marc' instead. It'll give you a chance to get comfortable with it."

So, the first time Jennifer used the name "Marc," it was with her therapist instead of her husband.

*****

Using the right pronouns proved even harder than using "Marc." It was so awkward! Telling someone that your wife is becoming your husband is hard enough, but trying to do it without saying the words "he" or "him" is nearly impossible. Jennifer thought about a conversation she'd had with Sandy, when trying to explain the situation. They were on a lunch break and Jen tried to open up as she picked at her salad.

"Well, Mar is still genetically female but presents as male." Jen took several swallows of water, wondering what it would be like to choke on a lettuce leaf. Death by Caesar salad. The chatter around them was loud and made personal conversation difficult. Silverware clattered, and several people applauded as the waiter dropped a tray of empty dishes.

"Like cross-dressing?" her co-worker asked, trying to understand and grateful for this rare glimpse into her friend's private life. They were in a deli near work; Jen had hoped the cacophony and the anonymity of the lunch crowd would make it easier to share. It didn't. It only made it noisier.

"Nooooo," Jen slowly answered, learning that patience was going to be required as she tried to help others understand this change. Of course, *she* didn't understand it, which didn't help matters.

"Mar is actually *physically* changing. Mar feels like Mar was born in the wrong body, and wants to become a man. Mar thinks that this will make Mar happy."

It felt like a script of out some sort of sit-com. Or the movie *Rain Man*. Nothing about it felt natural to Jennifer, including the pronouns. But no matter how awkward it sounded, she simply couldn't bring herself to refer to her wife as a "him" or a "he."

*****

The issue came up one night after they'd met up with friends from the radio station. Jen pulled into the driveway, narrowly missing the trashcan on the curb.

"It feels so weird when you use my name instead of pronouns," Mar said, and kind of laughed, as though they were discussing something as unimportant as the weirdo neighbor and her nine cats.

Jen had been trying so hard to deal with the situation as best she could but couldn't help lashing out. She shoved the car into park and snatched her keys from the ignition. "Well, it's better than using the wrong pronoun, isn't it? I'm *trying*!" she insisted. Without another word, she unbuckled her seat belt and left the car.

Left behind in the car, Marc felt bad. Jennifer *was* trying, and he saw how it was affecting her. He reminded himself he needed to be patient, that this was as much of a change for her as it was for him. Rubbing his eyes, Marc got out of the car and went to retrieve the wayward trashcan.

*****

In some ways, telling others served to make the transition easier on Jennifer. Hearing their friends call him "Marc" and use "he" and "him" made it more familiar, adding a level of comfort that Jennifer hadn't felt before. A visit from Marika's high school friend, Tom, was a turning point. They'd all gone out to dinner on the Eastern Shore, comfortably chatting and joking as always. Hearing Tom refer to Marc as "him" seemed to click things into place for Jen.

"We can't take him anywhere. He needs a babysitter," Tom joked to the waiter, who was mopping up after Marc knocked over his water glass. In the casual restaurant and with one of their closest friends, it sounded natural.

Jennifer caught herself using the correct pronouns more than once that night. She had finally been able to refer to her wife as a male. It was progress.

But making it a habit took a while.

"Mar was snoring, and he woke herself up!" Jen would share with someone. Or, "When she went to pay the bill, his coins spilled out all over the floor." Jennifer kept mixing up names and pronouns. It took her many months before she consistently got them right, and more than a year before she did it without thinking about it.

But as Jen fought to be comfortable with her choice of words, the anxiety was slowly building inside her—a ticking time bomb that was about to explode. It was a tale of two souls who couldn't have been at more opposite ends of self-acceptance. While Marika was exulting in becoming Marc, Jennifer was losing herself.

When the official notification of the name change came in the mail— the day Marika *officially* became Marc—Jennifer found solace by slicing her skin with a box cutter.

Chapter 7
The First Cut is the Deepest

Jennifer sat at her desk at work, trying to focus. But as usual, her brain refused to cooperate, instead spinning silently while mulling the continued litany of questions and non-answers. She'd begun thinking somehow maybe this was her fault. Self-doubt (always her constant companion) took on an almost human persona, creeping into every waking thought and hovering even as she tried to sleep.

The emotional stress was taking its toll. She missed work. She stopped wearing makeup. Getting out of bed required more and more effort. Even just opening her eyes took will power simply because it forced her brain to admit it was required to think again.

Her co-workers knew something was up but didn't know what or why. They just knew Jennifer—usually so even-keeled and reasonable—was acting irrationally. They talked about it in the break room, hushed voices filled with concern.

"Is Jen here today?" Mary Beth needed Jen's help with a file.

"Yeah, but she came in late again," Melissa answered.

"Oh God. At least Lydia had a flat tire so she was late too. Maybe she didn't notice."

"Do you know what's going on with her? She's acting so weird. I heard something was up with her wife. Is she sick?" Melissa was dying to know what was going on in the office.

Christy was shocked everyone didn't know the news. "You didn't hear? Her wife is having a sex change!"

"Are you kidding? What the hell? How wild!" Melissa almost seemed delighted at this news. It didn't affect her in any way but it sure did liven up her conversations.

It sounded like high school gossip, but it was so much more than inconsequential drama. It was a matter of life and death. Her co-workers were concerned about Jennifer and her well-being.

"She looks so sad," Mary Beth said.

"I asked her out for lunch but she turned me down. I wish I could get her to talk to me," Sandy said, sadly.

Melissa agreed. "I know. She's always so quiet. I can't believe she'd open up about something as personal as this."

Usually a solid employee, it was evident Jennifer was slipping up.

"Did you hear she lost the Dixon file?" Christy had always been one for gossip, even when it affected someone she cared about. She didn't mean it maliciously, she simply loved to share anything that resembled "dirt."

Melissa had heard their boss searching for it the day before. "I know. Lydia was furious."

"I just hope she doesn't get fired." Sandy worried about her friend who was clearly hurting so deeply.

And on and on. The talk never stopped. It wasn't catty; merely curious. Her co-workers were worried about her, but also casually flabbergasted at their friend's personal life. They wanted all the salacious details, things that weren't any of their business and never would be.

*****

Today, for some reason, was worse than usual. Anxious, nervous, the tension built until Jennifer felt she'd burst into a billion pieces. She imagined tiny bits of herself scattered throughout the office, her boss "tsking" as she tried to sweep them up with a dustpan, muttering, "She shoulda listened. I told her to keep her family life at home."

Trying to reign in her emotions, Jennifer balled her hands into fists and dug her fingernails into her palm. The nails created tiny half-moons in her skin, bisecting her life line. Or maybe it was her love line. Either one felt so off course at this point the bisection felt natural. And interestingly, the pain didn't hurt—instead, to her amazement, it provided momentary relief. Jennifer's anxiety ebbed a tiny bit, and she felt a brief sense that everything would be okay.

"Hey!" Mary Beth interrupted her thoughts, startling her. "Got lunch plans? I'm craving egg drop soup and some of us thought we could try out that new Chinese food place. Wanna?"

Jennifer tried to come up with a reasonable excuse, but she couldn't. She'd begged off so many times she'd run out of reasons to say no. Besides, she liked Mary Beth, and maybe getting out of the office would do her good. She wasn't really hungry, but she made up her mind to try to eat something.

"Yep, sure. Sounds good." Jen tried to smile brightly but really only managed a slight upturn. It was enough to pass, though. Mary Beth looked pleased.

"Cool. Just let me go grab my purse," she replied. "Meetcha in the lobby."

And as Mary Beth walked away to retrieve her bag, Jennifer glanced down at her palms. The marks from her nails were still there, and so was her belief that she and Marika (*Marc*, she thought, resolutely) could work things out. She smiled and left for lunch.

* * * * *

Over the next few days, Jen found that squeezing her hands really tightly helped her cope with the stress that stalked her like a crazed ex-lover. Multiple times each day, she closed her eyes and squeezed her hands with all her might, inwardly rejoicing as she marked her palms with those tiny half-moons at the end of her fingers. The relief it provided wasn't always equal (sometimes it lasted a minute or two, sometimes longer), but it always helped a little, at least. And it was enough.

Jen used it to cope with the stress of her commute home, releasing one hand from the steering wheel to squeeze tightly. And when Marika would bring up a topic Jennifer didn't want to discuss, she found it a decent, hidden method to control her emotions.

Until Sunday night. They were cooking dinner and superficial conversation filled the air.

"Don't forget we have to get the car inspected this week," said Jen, ever the organizer.

"Right. Oh, which reminds me, Deb has free tickets to the show on Friday, but we'd have to drive. I told her I'd see what you thought."

Jennifer focused on chopping the peppers for the stir-fry they were fixing as Marika prepared the chicken. The knife in Jen's hands blurred as she sliced the veggies in neat, even strips. *Slice.* Slide a pile of peppers out of the way. *Slice, slice, slice.* A colorful collection of red and green comma-shaped peppers slid on to the plate.

"Sure, sounds good. Mar, hand me the onion over there?"

Grabbing the onion, Marika's hand brushed Jen's as she handed it over. The tingle she'd once felt at her lover's touch was nonexistent. Jen peeled the outer layer away, preparing to slice the onion to match the peppers. *Slice.* She neatly halved and quartered it, totally focused on the task at hand.

"Hey, hon, would you try calling me Marc? I know I've only filled out the form so far, but my name change should be official pretty soon. I know it might feel kinda weird but I wish you'd try to use it once in a while, at least. It'll help us both get used to it."

Stab.

The knife stuck in the cutting board, blade first, as Jennifer whirled around to face her wife. She wasn't ready for this. Couldn't have this discussion. Couldn't yet accept that Marika was still determined to transition. Not yet. Why couldn't Marika understand? She. Wasn't. Ready.

Jennifer walked away without a word, the tip of the knife still buried in the cutting board.

*****

Monday morning found her broken. She forced herself to shower, punishing herself with the hottest water the old plumbing could produce, trying to scald the sadness she felt to her core. It didn't work. Jennifer arrived at work clean but no less emotionally enervated. The morning droned on as she replayed the scene in the kitchen.

Things she could have said flooded her mind.

"What if I said *I* wanted to become a man? What would you think about *that*?" or "How 'bout you try calling me something besides Jennifer? Do you think it'd be easy to make that change?"

But she'd kept quiet, as usual. It was easier not to fight. Less hurtful not to dig into it. She was the good girl, after all. The people pleaser. Ruffling feathers didn't come easy for her, no matter the circumstance. She balled up her anger, burying it deep inside.

*****

Jennifer neatly stacked the patient report she'd been working on and reached for the stapler, realizing only after she'd managed to put two tiny indentations in the pages that it was empty. Opening her desk drawer, the overhead office light glinted off the perfect row of staples waiting for her to refill the empty stapler. The idea flashed across her mind in a split-second. She took in the tiny pointed tips of each staple, eyeing them as though she'd never seen them before. Suddenly it seemed so obvious.

Jen removed one staple from the row, delicately handling it as though it were a flower. She marveled at its sleekness, its size, in disbelief she hadn't ever considered how impactful it could be. This one innocuous little staple held the power to make her feel better. How had she not noticed?

She gently picked it up between her thumb and forefinger, drawing it across the back of her hand. Gently first, then more firmly. The ribbon of blood followed quickly then, reflecting the same office light as it glinted in the florescent glow. She felt relief instantly course through her veins even as the blood struggled out of them along the scratch. Jennifer smiled.

*****

Marc was feeling a different euphoria. His name change was official and he was no longer bound by a birth name that hadn't ever felt right. *Marc.* That felt right. Comfortable. Marc couldn't wait to celebrate this enormous milestone with Jen. He'd already called to tell her the news. Jennifer hadn't said much on the phone, but now that he was home they could talk through it, maybe even go out to dinner to mark the occasion. Bounding up the stairs, Marc called out to her.

*****

Jennifer sat with the blade in hand. Maybe her mother had been right all along. Maybe she *couldn't* handle it. She flashed back to how many times she'd consoled her mom, both of them in Cindy's room with its floral wallpaper—airy almost to the point of ethereal. It was meant to feel like a sanctuary, an escape from the real world. But how often had Cindy, in the throes of depression, lain in there and wept? Jennifer would sit with her time and again, trying to offer comfort and compassion, continually feeling she'd failed at both.

She'd failed again.

*****

"Jen? Jennifer? Hey, babe, let's celebrate!" Hearing no response, Marc checked the bedroom but Jen wasn't waiting there. He walked down the hall to the guest bedroom, which was empty. The kitchen showed no sign of meal prep underway. *Where is she?* he wondered.

Marc continued his search for his wife. He'd checked both bedrooms and the kitchen. Maybe she was in the bathroom.

Just a glimpse into the tiny bath showed the whole scene in a tragic second: Jen, bloody and strangely sedate, sitting very still on the seat. Marc was stunned, momentarily mesmerized by the sight.

"What the hell? What happened?" he shouted. Marc's eyes went from the bleeding stripes on Jen's leg to the box cutter in her hand, still dripping with the evidence of what she'd done. It took a moment for the reality to sink in. She was calm, almost trancelike. He was anything but.

"Oh, my God!" he screamed.

He moved quickly then, grabbing towels to mop up the blood and coaxing Jen to help him clean her wounds, hurriedly wrapping her leg in a makeshift bandage. Five cuts neatly lined her thigh. This was no accident. Moments later, Marc was on the phone to Jen's therapist.

"Jackie? Hey, it's Marik—Marc. Jennifer's ..." In the moment, he was so shaken even he wasn't sure what to say. "... husband," he finally got out. "Jen's cut herself really badly. On purpose!"

Jackie heard the fear. "Okay, where did she cut herself? Can you move her?"

"Her leg. It's awful. I can't tell how deep. But I can help her get to the car."

"Take her to the ER. The doctors there'll know what to do."

It was the first but not the only time Marc called her about self-injury.

*****

It took hours before they were seen. Magazines littered the tables beside the hard, vinyl-covered furniture that stuck to exposed skin like tape to a wall. Changing position on the industrial-style chair threatened to remove a layer of dermis with it. Finding comfort was a lost cause. It was functional at best.

The clock on the wall ticked the seconds off loudly. *Chk, chk, chk.* The sound echoed in the crowded waiting room, noticeable above the noise of those who waited in pain, in fear, in disbelief at whatever tragedy had brought them in. Accident victims, those sick with flu, a woman badly beaten by her husband—they all sat in this vinyl-covered purgatory waiting in anonymous solidarity.

As she sat next to Marc, Jen had a chance encounter with a co-worker from the cardiologist's office. Sonia had come in with her sick daughter and was on her way out when she saw Jennifer sitting to the side.

"Hey there! You okay?" Sonia asked.

Jen had zoned out, still dazed by what she'd done. It took her a moment to realize someone was talking to her, longer still to recognize the speaker.

"Oh, hi. Uh, yeah. I am. Or I will be," she responded, more out of routine than out of belief in what she was saying.

"I, um, had an accident with a box cutter."

"Oh my God! Are you okay? Let me see—where is it?"

Jen demurred. It was just the first of many times that question would be asked that night.

*****

For some stupid reason, everyone wanted to see her cuts. The receptionist who checked them in. The nurse who first tended to her in the ER. The doctor on call who needed to determine whether she needed stitches. Jennifer refused them all. These were *her* cuts, *her* private marks. No one was going to see.

The nurses called her back and examined her. Then it was the doctor's turn. Having determined her wounds were self-inflicted, he called someone from psych to come see Jennifer. Dr. Whatever-her-name-was (Jen wasn't really paying attention. She didn't care) was very firm—the only way she'd let Jennifer go home that night was to reveal the damage. Jen felt a strange satisfaction as she unwound the bandage Marc had wrapped around her leg before they left the house.

Satisfaction was only part of it. Jen felt ... euphoric. As though nothing and no one would ever bring her down again. She was on a high like nothing she'd ever imagined. *This must be what runners talk about*, she thought. *And I didn't even have to get sweaty to feel it*. She nearly grinned at her own joke but stopped when the stupid psych person (*Or was that psycho*, she thought) pushed a paper in front of her, demanding her signature.

"What's this?" Jen and Marc both asked simultaneously.

"This," Dr. Whatever-her-name-was said somewhat pretentiously, "tells us you're not going to do this again. That before you'd ever harm yourself, you'll come back here and talk to us first."

Jen nearly laughed out loud: partly at the absurdity that a form would keep her from doing it again, and partly because the whole damn evening had been so surreal. *Who's gonna come back?* she thought, and picked up the pen to sign.

*****

Marc was surprised they let Jennifer go home. And scared. It was up to him to make sure it didn't happen again. They went home, both agreeing to take the next day off work to talk through what happened.

That day was quiet, somber. Both of them cocooned in the house, going about their daily routines that felt anything but normal. Cooking breakfast, drinking coffee, reading emails. Finally, Marc broached the subject.

"Can you help me understand why?" he pleaded.

Jen tried. "I guess it's just ... it felt good." She realized how ridiculous that sounded even as she said the words, but it was true. It *had* felt good.

"When you called, when you said your name change was official, I don't know... it just reminded me that I have no control over any of this. You're making the decisions, you're changing our future, and I'm ... I'm supposed to just go along with it." Her eyes were downcast, embarrassed to meet his. Unused to asserting herself, this was new territory for Jennifer.

Marc reached out for her hand. Jen took it, giving it a squeeze. He cleared his throat. He didn't want to say the next words but knew he had to—he had to make sure she knew she had options. He couldn't blame her if this was too much. "Babe, I gotta say this. I hope you will stay. I really do. I would hate it if you left me, but I get it. This isn't what you signed up for when we got married."

"No, it isn't. I don't want to leave, but I also don't know if I can stay. I love you. I just wish I could be okay with this. Like, if I could just shrug my shoulders and say, 'Okay, this is how it is.' But I can't."

"I get that. I do." He felt guilty as hell for making her so unhappy. She felt guilty for making him feel bad. There was plenty of guilt to go around.

As the pair opened up, each trying to make the other feel better, the doorbell rang.

Jen's parents stood on the other side of it.

*****

As it turned out, Jen's mom, Cindy, had picked that day of all days to spontaneously drop by her office for a visit. Sonia, the co-worker who'd seen Jennifer in the hospital, explained to her mother what Jen had told her. Jennifer's mother wasted no time in picking up her father and coming to see her.

"Honey, what happened?" Jen's mom asked almost before the door was shut. "I stopped to see you at work and they told me you'd been cut! Why didn't you call? It was so bad you had to go to the hospital? What happened?"

The questions rained down like a summer thunderstorm in all its fury, pelting Marc and Jen until they almost physically felt each and every query stinging them. Everyone was talking all at once, except Jen's dad who stood silently, taking in the scene.

Marc started. "If you'll just wait a min—

Jen also attempted to explain. "Mom, let me—

"I shouldn't have to hear from a CO-WORKER that you were in the HOSPITAL," Cindy's voice powered over all of them.

The room got quiet. Jen drew a deep breath and suggested they all sit down. Marc offered to get drinks for everyone, hoping to escape the tension. Jennifer's parents declined drinks but sat, awkwardly trying to regain some sense of composure.

They were scattered across the room like checkers, strategically placed for strength in what was to come. Jen's parents on one side, she and Marc on the other. Unplanned, it was a face off. Marc grabbed a pen on the table next to him and fidgeted with it, his nervous energy palpable.

Jennifer started the conversation this time, calmly explaining what she'd done to herself. It was odd, really—as she was retelling it, it was almost as though she were talking about someone else taking a box cutter and slicing their own skin. "...and I just kept making cuts, one right next to the other, trying to make them evenly spaced," Jen said plainly.

She relived it as she relayed it: the feel of the blade, the scent of her blood, the feeling of complete and utter intoxication without a drop of alcohol. Her parents looked on, horrified, as she recounted the events of the previous evening as though she were sharing nothing more important than a recipe for Bundt cake. Guessing (correctly) that her parents would blame Marc, Jennifer tried to diffuse the condemnation.

"Marc was great, though. He called the doctor, he got me to the hospital. He was right with me the whole time." She smiled at him, grateful for his presence both last night and during this stressful conversation. He offered a small smile back.

Jen wrapped up the story by explaining that they'd taken the day off work to talk through it all and move forward.

"Move forward?" Jen's mom asked incredulously. "How can you 'move forward?' You CUT yourself, Jennifer!"

Like I forgot, Jen thought.

"You don't move forward. You move home, out of here, and away from this place. You come home," Cindy said.

It was an order, not an invitation. And Jen wasn't having it. "Mom, I am not moving home. I'm staying here. I don't know how all of this is going to go, but I love her and she loves me and we're going to try to make this work. She couldn't do it, couldn't say his name yet. "I love her and she loves me and we're going to try to make this work."

"But she—he—whatever—is the reason you're hurting! You're hurting so much YOU CUT YOURSELF! You can't stay here. You can't handle this!" Cindy blurted out.

And there it is, Jennifer thought. Jen thought about her mother's ongoing issues with self-esteem due to her lifelong battle with her weight and, in part, Cindy's relationship with her own mom. Cindy had (without meaning to, of course) projected her own insecurities onto her daughter. She truly believed she wasn't good at anything, which of course, wasn't true. Hearing Cindy say it again and again about herself, Jennifer felt compelled to disagree—to help her mom see some good within. It never worked and usually left Jen feeling like she couldn't do enough to help.

Jennifer remembered sitting next to her mom often as her mother wept during one depressive bout, unable to find the words that would convince Cindy she was worthy and leaving Jen feeling inadequate. Cindy felt incapable of handling anything stressful, as though it might break her emotionally. For some reason, Cindy felt that if she couldn't handle something, her daughter wouldn't be able to either. "You can't handle this. It's too much," became a mantra Cindy repeated over and over to Jennifer regarding anything from an overly full schedule to wanting to change college majors. Fortunately, Jennifer didn't believe it. Most of the time.

******

Cindy looked directly at Marc. "This is YOUR fault, you know!"

That was the breaking point for Jennifer. She didn't understand Marc's decision any more today than she had yesterday, but she wouldn't let her parents blame him. "This conversation is over, Mom. It's over. I'm not talking about this anymore with you, and I'm not coming with you. I'm staying here, in my home. And if you're going to be here, you're going to have to stop blaming Mar ... her ... for everything that's happened. *I did it to myself, Mom. ME. Not anyone else. It's no one's fault but my own!*"

Cindy processed that quietly for a moment, gathering her thoughts. "Jennifer, I'm not going to sit here and say I'm not concerned. I am. I'm very concerned. You can't blame me for that." She pulled at the hem of her skirt, then picked off an imaginary piece of lint as she braced herself to ask the next question.

"Can I see them? The cuts?" she asked.

Why is that so damned important to everyone? Jen wondered. *Does she think she can assess how damaged I am by how bad the wound is?*

Jennifer didn't comply. Instead, she ended the visit, convincing her parents she was fine. She told them about the form she'd signed, saying she'd go back to the hospital if she had any more thoughts of hurting herself. She ushered them out with a sigh of relief, as ready to close the door on her hurt as she was her parents' blame.

******

Sadly, this scene would play out time and again—Jennifer cutting to relieve her anxiety, Marc doing his best to relieve her pain, both physical and emotional. Jen found razors at work and smuggled some to the house to continue her self-mutilation.

Sometimes she cut daily; sometimes she could go a bit longer between. Usually it wasn't bad enough to send her to the hospital. She cut at home, at work, at dance classes. Razor blades. Box cutters. Once it was a kitchen knife. Each sharp object served the purpose she sought—relieving the pressure. Mostly she cut her right leg and left forearm. And, as she had that first time, often she made an uneven number of cuts. It was a ritualistic act and for some unknown reason, the odd number soothed her.

******

Bleed

let it drip, let it flow
let it spill, pour, drain
out of me.

let me bleed until I am empty

until there's nothing left to give
write my story in pain, and blood
tell it well

tell them how you found me
how pale and snowy white
tell them how at peace I looked
tell them I am happy now.

don't cry or grieve
I had already ceased to exist
I had already died inside
I was already gone
maybe you didn't notice
maybe you just ignored the signs
perhaps you didn't care enough;
Or cared too much, you were blind to it
to me, to my pain, to my screams of red

let my blood red tears, and screams
of pain, of exhaustion, of anger and rage
let it tell the story of how I was too weak
of how I couldn't go on

let it tell them I was lost
let it say how I was lonely
alone, solitary
confined by my own emotion
torn by my own hand

tell them this is what I wanted
let my heart go
no tears, no pain, no rage where I am now
don't you know I was empty
the blood emptied my body
as my heart was emptied by life

this life was not for me
it wasn't meant to be
i wasn't free here
i was a prisoner of my own head
now i can soar
i see you
i can see you looking at my body
at my blood
holding me close, warmed by my newly drained blood
you touch your face, and your tears mix with my blood.

******

Doctors prescribed Xanax hoping to ease Jen's anxiety. Ironically, it served to lower her inhibitions—making it easier for her to engage in self-mutilation. At some point during this cycle, the high that Jen felt after cutting—that euphoric calm that followed the act—lessened. Each time, she had to go deeper, cut more, to feel relief that lasted for a shorter and shorter period of time. As the pain intensified, so did Jen's desire for numbness. She didn't want to feel, didn't want to think, didn't want to have to consider the future. Numb, she wouldn't have to. About a year after she made that first cut, she took things too far.

*****

Jen had decided to move out of the bedroom she and Marc shared. She needed space and thought it might help her make sense of the thoughts that constantly swirled around her head and give her some clarity about their situation.

As Marc napped downstairs, Jennifer carefully arranged things in the upstairs guest room: her favorite lamp next to the bed, the framed picture of her in her final dance recital. It was all just as she liked it, everything in its place. She looked at the freshly made bed with satisfaction—she could make it each morning and know that it would stay nicely made without Marc there to mess it up.

Maybe I should've moved out of our room a while ago, she thought, cynically.

The satisfaction she felt went beyond appreciating the orderliness of the room. It was an anticipation of sorts. She had planned her afternoon out already—looking forward to going into the bathroom, shutting the door, and cutting. Jen felt the good kind of nerves that people felt before riding a roller coaster or going on a first date: hopeful, excited, and expectant. Ever the planner, she'd even laid out the Xanax to take afterwards so she could drift off into peaceful oblivion. The glass of water sat next to the small white pills like a trusted friend—patiently waiting until it was needed to ease her transition to sleep.

With a last glance at the bed (the top corner of the sheets already pulled back, welcoming her return and inviting her to easily slide under them), Jen made her way to the bathroom for her ritual. The cutting had become more than a way to relieve anxiety; it actually made her *feel* something. She'd had become so deadened to her emotions that taking a sharp object to her skin allowed her to feel alive again.

That feeling became reinforcing, leaving Jen nearly powerless to stop repeating her self-injurious deed. In execution, it was almost like bursting a huge bubble that allowed her to release the pain that built inside her.

*****

Whether she recognized it or not (she didn't), guilt had been part of Jennifer's life for much of her life. It crept upon her stealthily, in myriad ways, without her noticing.

Her mother, without meaning to, had contributed to it. Cindy's long-time battle with depression had cast a pall over the house throughout Jen's younger years. Jennifer tried so hard to help her mother. Her inability to "fix" her mom, to make her feel better during each of her depressive episodes, left her spent and feeling useless. Eventually it was too draining, and she stopped trying. Her resignation to Cindy's condition added to the guilt Jennifer felt.

*****

Jennifer entered the tiny bathroom to recover the razor blade she'd smuggled home from work. Marc kept finding her stashes of blades, but she prided herself on finding new places to hide them. She'd taped this one inside the top of the toilet tank, and he hadn't thought to search there yet. Proud of her ingenuity, Jen picked up the blade.

*****

Pain

Up and down
Side to side
Attacking at every angle
Diagonally striking
I swerve to miss.
Duck to survive
Bend backwards trying to dodge.

But it hits
Bombards my brain
Invades my heart
Poisons my emotions
Deteriorates my body

I can't stop it,
Can't hide from it.
When I run it only pursues faster
Racing at the speed of light
Catching me, trapping me.
I trip,
I fall,
I don't know how long I will be down.

Minutes, hours, days?
Time passes slowly
Unpredictable
Uncontrollable,
I am misunderstood.
It's me, not you.

I bleed it out
But it always returns.
I burn its core
But it flares up again
And again.

There's no escape.
No way out.
Is there a secret passage
A hidden exit?
Will I find it in time
To save my body?

* * * * *

Jennifer instantly knew this time it was bad. She'd made the cut on the top of her right thigh, just as she had so many times before, but this one went longer, deeper than she'd intended. Immediately queasy, she yelled for her husband.

"Marc! MARC!!" Somehow the name—complete with the 'c'—escaped easily from her lips. Jennifer didn't notice. She was fixated on the blood gushing from her thigh, a bright red river already overflowing its banks and spilling onto the bathroom floor. Her vision swam.

Footsteps pounded up the stairs but her voice stopped him.

"Don't come upstairs!" she screamed. "I'm coming down. We need to go to the ER. Get the car!"

Jennifer summoned everything within her to tear her eyes away from the wound, forcing herself to stand. The gash she'd made mocked her, taunting her to try to walk. She managed to make her way to the stairs. Sliding down them was easier, and again, Jennifer's eyes were drawn to the red stripe leaving a trail of blood in her wake, a reminder of the psychic pain she'd felt and released only moments ago, now morphing into nearly unbearable physical pain.

*****

Marc nearly vomited when he saw Jen stumbling to the front door. He'd seen her other self-injuries often enough to know this one was different: longer and dangerously deep. Despite their physical difference in size, he half-carried her to the car, unable to bring himself to ask her what she'd done. He knew, and he felt inordinately guilty to think he could have had anything to do with why she was in such physical and mental pain.

*****

The hospital staff jumped into action when they saw them approach, whisking both of them back to an ER room without asking questions or handing Jennifer the dreaded forms to fill out first. It was evident she needed immediate attention.

They were put in an ER bay they'd never been in before but the sterile environment of the small room was familiar: the gleaming silver clock monotonously counting off seconds; the counter cleared of all but the necessary glass containers of cotton balls, tongue depressors, and antiseptic swabs. Labeled drawers neatly contained everything else the staff would need to attend to emergency patients. If she hadn't been so focused on her injury, Jennifer would've appreciated the neatness of the room. Instead, both she and Marc sat silently waiting for the doctor to come in, absorbed in their own tortured thoughts about what brought them to the hospital. Again.

In a relatively short time (because hospital time is its own algorithm that doesn't follow any clock in the real world—every minute in a hospital seems to take ten "real-world" minutes), the doctor walked in. Professional but personable, his brown hair swooped to one side giving him a kind of David Beckham air. He grabbed her chart, briefly took a look at her wound and joked. "You did a really good job on this." Likely just out of residency, the doc assumed Jen had had some sort of accident, not yet understanding she'd intentionally held the blade to cleave her thigh. His joke fell flat. Jennifer refused to meet Marc's eyes.

"That's a whopper of a cut, but we'll get you stitched up here in no time," he continued, not picking up on—or perhaps casually ignoring—that the tension in the room had just ratcheted up several notches after his offhanded humor. Calling for the nurse to prepare the needle with a numbing agent, he tried to make small talk as he got ready to suture her laceration. Jen sat miserably silent, lost in self-flagellation.

"A pretty impressive wound," he said, appreciatively. "So, how'd it happen?" He skillfully threaded the suturing needle as though he were preparing to hem a pair of pants.

Jennifer was mute. After a longer than normal pause, Marc answered for her. Four little words that spelled out the enormity of what was going on. "It was self-inflicted."

The doctor said nothing, but if either Jen or Marc had been watching closely they'd have seen his eyes narrow for just a split second before he caught himself. Realizing the ridiculousness of his earlier attempt at humor, he joined in the awkward hush that engulfed the room. Fortunately, the nurse came bustling in just then, breaking both the tension and the silence as she injected Jennifer with Lidocaine to numb the area for stitches.

Marc reached for Jen's hand as the doctor started sewing the gash closed, one precise stitch at a time. Jennifer forced herself to count each time the needle pierced her flesh, neatly and precisely moving in and out, a whipstitch that sewed her body instead of a skirt. Twenty-two stitches later, the doctor was done and stood back to see his work.

"I'm going to need to call someone to come and talk to you," he said. While the words "psych department" didn't come out of his mouth, both Marc and Jen knew who that someone would be.

The short wait they'd experienced when they arrived was not repeated. This waiting period was long and unbearably slow (even in real time, never mind hospital minutes), and there was little talk between them. Neither knew what to say. At last the psychiatrist on call came, and Jennifer felt an eerie familiarity as the conversation closely followed a strangely similar route as that first night she'd cut herself.

Oddly, they let her leave (but only after signing that same, absurd form promising to come in when she felt the urge to use a blade on her own skin). 'Cause that worked so well, Jennifer thought wryly. It was the worst of her self-inflicted injuries and one of the last. But Jennifer wasn't done hurting herself; she just chose another method.

*****

(untitled)

i am alone.
There are people all around
and i am alone.
i am talking to you
and i am alone.
You are holding my hand
and i am alone.
You are there when i fall asleep,
You are there when i wake
and i am alone.
You sit there telling me i am not alone
and i am alone.
i am more alone surrounded by people
than i am by myself.
i am less alone with my own thoughts
than i am when you are speaking.
And i am alone.

******

Jennifer moved back into their bedroom, shutting the door both literally and figuratively on the guest bedroom and the heart-wrenching episode that transpired within its walls. And while they went about their days together sharing a life, a home and a bed, they talked. They went on dates. They attended therapy together and separately, delving deep into their psyches to find the common ground they'd once taken for granted. They did it all together, Jennifer and Marc, steadfastly facing a future that still seemed as uncertain as it had before that watershed day when Marc announced he wanted to transition. They were a couple, and they poured their souls into keeping it that way.

And as Marc prepared to take the next step—testosterone shots—Jennifer had never felt more forsaken.

Chapter 8
Marc

It was summer, and the couple drove north to Philadelphia, where Marc would get his first shot at the Mazzoni Center. Jen sat resolutely by his side, not saying much but doing her best to show support. She'd decided that if Marc was going to do this, she was going with him.

The car was warmed by the July sun, a moving microwave on wheels baking the two humans inside. Jen put the window down and let the fresh air blow through her hair. The rushing noise helped fill the car with sound, masking the quiet that both pretended not to notice.

Marc was excited and anxious. He'd done his homework, researching the various ways to pursue hormone therapy. Each had pros and cons, but Marc had decided on testosterone shots. Pills were available and would be equally effective, but he'd read they'd been proven to be pretty hard on the kidneys and liver. Shots it was.

Marc would get a shot every other week to facilitate his transition to a man, relying on the hormone to do everything from lowering his voice to stopping menses.

They took the exit for downtown Philadelphia, turning on to Locust Street and looking for a parking place. After maneuvering the car into a parallel spot, Marc turned off the engine and turned to Jennifer.

"Thank you," he said, simply.

"I haven't done anything," Jen answered, somewhat quizzically.

"You're here," he said back, and leaned over to kiss her.

Seatbelts off, they climbed out of the car. Jennifer took his hand as they headed toward the building.

*****

Inside, they walked through a maze of hallways to find the doctor's office. Marc's appointment was for 10:30. They were early.

As they waited, Jen flipped through the magazines and pamphlets on the table. Marc, true to form, flipped his phone around in circles, unable to sit still. They weren't *not* talking, but neither had much to say. Marc was too preoccupied with what was about to happen, Jen wrapped up in her own thoughts and emotions. Questions came to mind fast and furiously, pelting her like insects assaulting a light, too fast for her to settle on any of them: *How did we get here? How on earth is this going to play out? How long can I stay? Do I still want to?*

The nurse came in to get them. "Hi, Marc. You ready?"

"I am!" He jumped to his feet, eager to get started. Jennifer stood as well without the same exuberance. She looked at her wife, memorizing every feature and wishing she could freeze time so that face would never change.

"Let's go, then," Jen said, and took Marc's hand. It was time to begin.

The first noticeable change was the acne. Flaring up across his face, Marc looked like he was going through puberty all over again. An acne garden in full bloom replaced the smooth skin he'd taken for granted for the past dozen or so years—ever since he'd gone through adolescence the first time. Being Marc, he joked it off as best he could, naming his zits and poking fun at his pizza face.

The voice change was next, and took longer to manifest. For a while, people probably thought he had a cold. His timbre was slightly lower and kind of raspy. Not manly yet but not the female voice that once blanketed the airwaves either. It wasn't overly noticeable except for the occasional telltale crack as the larynx strained. It would be months before his voice settled into a lower register once and for all. Those who talked to Marc regularly didn't notice much; the change was pretty gradual. But Marc could hear the difference and welcomed the more masculine sound.

One of the most noticeable—and faster—changes was fat distribution. The testosterone worked its magic pretty quickly, slimming Marc's hips and buttocks to result in a manlier physique. His breasts were still there but he started wearing a binder to flatten them and they were unnoticeable under the tight wrap.

It took a few months before he noticed the hair, but there it was—arm and leg hair coming in darker and coarser than it ever had.

The facial hair took the longest, which meant that with his round face, oily skin, and super short haircut, Marc resembled an androgynous teen not sure of their sexuality.

Strangers weren't sure either: is that a guy? A girl? Marc would laugh when the server at a new restaurant would say "sir" or "mister." They didn't say it as though they were quite certain; it was more of a question. Marc thought it was hysterical.

*****

At the Mazzoni Center, the doctor had shown Marc how to give himself the testosterone shots. Jen had watched closely, curious to see this simple act that was about to impact their lives so drastically. The night she asked if she could do it for him, she caught him off guard.

"*You* want to give me my shot?" Marc asked.

"Yeah, if that's okay. Maybe it'll make me feel better about this. Like I have a part in all of it," she answered. It made sense, and Marc was more than happy to see her volunteer.

Jennifer followed him into the bathroom where he kept his supplies in the medicine cabinet. She'd seen the doctor do it, of course, but she listened as Marc told her what to do—glad to have a moment to bond with him over it.

The bathroom was tiny, with barely enough room to stand outside of the shower. Marc propped a leg up on the edge of the tub, while Jennifer sat on the toilet with his rear end literally in her face. They laughed at the absurdity of the position; it helped ease the tension.

"It's super thick, so you gotta be patient while you're filling the syringe," he reminded her. She smiled. She'd remembered that from the hospital, but she also knew what her willingness to give him the shot meant to him. She wasn't about to do anything to change the mood.

"Got it." Jen drew the plunger up, the thick liquid slowly following as though being coaxed. He'd already shown her how to swab the area with rubbing alcohol—now it was a matter of getting the right amount of fluid.

"To this line here?" She asked, holding it up so she could verify the amount. She was pretty certain she knew the answer but wanted to make sure.

"Yep, that's it," he answered.

"You ready, babe?" She took a breath. And with a quick jab and a very slow release (it was *really* thick liquid), she gave her first injection.

*****

Each day brought more changes to his body. Minute and mostly unnoticeable, they were there nonetheless. And over time, they added up, gradually altering his appearance.

Marc videotaped his transition, filming himself once a week or so. Because his body changed daily, the videos served to help him see, over time, just how much he'd changed. To those who saw him each day, like Jennifer, the evolution was easy to miss. Those who saw him after a few months commented on how different he looked.

"Nice whiskers, bud."

"You look thinner." (He did—his hips were one of the first things to go.)

It was all in the perspective.

Jennifer could tell he was disappointed that his breasts didn't change with the hormones. Outside of that he was clearly pleased to see his body morphing, but for years, the binder would prove to be a constant reminder of his former identity.

As Marc's appearance changed, Jen had been afraid that she'd feel like she was living with a stranger. From that perspective, the slow transformation was a very good thing. It made it a tiny bit easier to take the whole situation. Each day, her wife was just slowly a little less Marika and a little more Marc. It bought her some time to come to terms with the transition. She'd promised herself from the beginning she'd take this day by day and see how things went. Marc (Marika back then) had repeatedly assured her that he'd understand if she needed to leave. He wouldn't have blamed her in the least, but he was so grateful she was willing to at least try to see how it played out. He realized how very fortunate he was that she hadn't just given up immediately.

Interestingly, the changes to his body were only one part of Marc's transition. They were certainly the most noticeable, but other crucial things were at play. For instance, there was the question of which bathroom to use when they were out in public. Early in his transition, Marc often vacillated about whether to use the men's or the ladies' room. While he *felt* like a man, he didn't yet really *look* like one, and Jen watched his anxiety rise each time he needed to use the restroom because he was afraid of others' reactions. On the surface, it might seem like an inconsequential decision but it was potentially a dangerous one. They'd both heard horror stories about trans people being assaulted for something as simple as using the bathroom facility they identified with.

The issue came to a head one morning when they stopped at Panera for breakfast.

"Man, I really need to pee," Marc complained as they stood in line. He been agonizing over this since he realized he needed to go when they were only halfway to the restaurant.

"So go." Jen's snippy response mirrored her mood. She hadn't slept well and her edginess showed.

"I'm not sure ... do you think I should try the men's room? There's only one stall in there." Marc, of course, couldn't use the urinal. If someone was already using the stall, he'd have to walk out and go into the women's bathroom instead, which he knew would feel really awkward.

"Not my problem," was Jen's answer. It wasn't as though she didn't care. She was simply not in the frame of mind to be sympathetic at the moment.

Marc chose the men's room and lucked out: the stall was available.

The question of which restroom to use grew easier to answer with time. As his appearance became more masculine, Marc chose the men's room more frequently until it was a given that he'd use it every time.

The *apprehension* over using it was a different matter. In the back of both of their minds, the possibility of violence remained. It lessened, though, the more Marc grew into his new body. He became more comfortable as his appearance matched his mindset.

******

As the pieces of himself were falling into place one by one, Marc had never felt better about his decision to transition. In fact, he shared the videos that showed his body morphing, posting them on YouTube to allow friends and family that lived far away to keep up with his journey.

Jennifer tried to support Marc as best she could. She really did. She worked on getting comfortable using male pronouns to talk about her spouse. She gamely attempted to use the name "Marc" but often fell short. She watched as the love of her life became more at ease with his new body, and she vowed—often—that she'd get there herself.

Give it time, she thought. *You're just not ready yet.* And while she still took things a day at a time regarding the future of her marriage, she stayed. She never gave up hope that she'd get to a point where she could accept her wife as a man. She only knew she wasn't there yet. But as the testosterone succeeded, two more things were affected: her anxiety skyrocketed, and so did Marc's guilt.

He had no idea how that guilt was about to increase, or what was at stake as a result of his transition.

Chapter 9
Breathe

Breathe

My body aches
my head spins
my thoughts race,
and I struggle to catch my breath

everything is moving too fast
relax…I tell myself
but I can't
my muscles get tighter
I am caught in a bubble

everything outside myself has been muted
has been paused
I am alone in this torture
I am twisted up inside
tied in knots
someone has rearranged all of my organs

everything is wrong, inside and out
nothing looks or feels like it should
I can't escape the feelings that come
I can't escape the pain

it circles outside my bubble,
ready to invade
I can't leave this place or it will attack

how long will the walls withstand
how long can I hold them up
I am not strong enough to stay here forever
I am weaker all the time
the pain will win
it will permeate my skin, my heart, my soul

the blood sucking feelings will leave me hollow
void of all my cells, all my organs, all my tissues
a shell will remain
the skin will start to fall away from the bone
and I will cease to exist
nothing left
but the space
the wide empty space that my body used to consume
a hole
an abyss
a void

will anyone notice the void
if no one notices, is it a void at all
no one hears my screams
sees my tears
feels my pain
no one wants to save me
help me
they only torture me and kill me
with venomous words and blank stares

I see how you look at me
like I am a freak
like I am to blame
like I am the guilty one
I see it, and I wish I never had
I wish this didn't happen
I hope it will end soon

I can't go back
I can't more forward
quicksand is my life
stuck
wounded
unable to nourish myself
unable to heal
unable to move

here I am!
do you see me?
hear me?
feel me?
care for me?

I don't think you do
I don't think you want to
I think you wish me dead
away from you
invisible
I want that too
more than you
more than I even know
it's with me all the time

that wish
that hope
that prayer for sleep over wake
for death over life
it lives inside my mind, my heart, my soul.

Chapter 10
Cutting Doesn't Go Deep Enough

Jennifer looked at the scale again. That couldn't be right. She'd gained six pounds since they got married two years ago. She decided then and there she'd do something about it. And come time to make her New Year's resolutions, she did.

*****

It started innocently enough. Counting calories, measuring portions, weighing food. Both the scale and her body complied, shedding the unwanted pounds. It gave Jennifer a sense of confidence again. She knew her goal weight looked good on her 5'8" frame, and that made her feel good. Maybe she'd just lose a few more pounds to make sure she had a little wiggle room, in case the weight crept back on down the road.

"Hey honey, can you hand me that shirt?" she asked Marc one morning.

"That's nice. New?" he said, handing it over.

"Yeah, I needed something a little smaller, so I went shopping. You like?" she asked him, modeling it flirtatiously. She felt sexier now that she was back in control over her size.

"Yeah, I do. Looks good!" Marc offered the affirmation she craved.

Jennifer added exercise to her daily routine. She rode her bike all over the area, doing thirteen miles a day after work. Blonde hair streaming behind her, the wind, the sun, even the rain refreshed her—freedom on wheels. It became sort of a meditation for her—mile after mile melting pound after pound. She was literally and figuratively in the driver's seat, controlling her destination for the first time in years. The liberation she felt was exhilarating.

Marc noticed as more weight came off. The six pounds became ten, then fifteen. He took in her eating habits: 100-calorie snacks that served as meals, the lowest-calorie yogurt Jen could find counting as breakfast.

"Babe, I'm a little worried about you. Are you eating enough?" he'd gently ask. "I've got some leftover spaghetti. Want some?"

"No, I'm good. I'm not hungry. But thanks." She gave him a kiss to let him know she meant it and that she appreciated him looking out for her.

Truth was, she *was* hungry. But with her hunger came conflict. She liked feeling those pangs because it meant she was eating less, but the constant rumbling of her body requesting more food was uncomfortable. She could eat to make that feeling go away, but then she wouldn't lose weight. *It's a slippery slope, this losing weight thing,* she thought more than once. She had no idea how right she was.

When she started another set of exercises, she focused on the reward. The slim body she'd been blessed with, emerging from beneath the extra weight. She remembered one particular conversation with her mom when Cindy was bemoaning her own appearance.

"You are so lucky," Cindy had said wistfully. "You can eat anything you want and stay so skinny. You definitely got your father's genes. You'll never have to worry about being fat."

Winsome, slender Jennifer had heard it before. Her mom had always fought the scale. Jen never saw her as fat; she was just Mom. But she knew her mother had battled her weight all of her life. Watching how much energy Cindy put into trying to lose weight, Jen thought that being overweight must be the very worst thing in the world. She made up her mind at a very young age she'd never let that happen.

Given her new focus, Jen tricked herself into making food last as long as possible. If she could drag out the time it took to eat something, she'd stay full longer. She'd cube up an apple into the smallest bites she could, slowly chewing each small morsel to satisfy her need to eat. A single Granny Smith could take an hour to eat. Individual bags of popcorn (without butter or salt that would make her retain fluid and bump up the number on the scale) constituted an entire meal, one fluffy kernel at a time.

Jennifer's goal was to eat no more than 1,000 calories a day. Most days, she succeeded.

Of course, sometimes they ate out. If she'd been good up to that point in the day, she'd treat herself to a "bigger" meal, which meant indulging in a salad or a selection off the restaurant's light menu.

Months passed by and pounds melted off. By May, Jennifer knew she was in trouble; this was not normal behavior, yet she seemed powerless to stop it. Her psychiatrist, Dr. Dorian, noticed her weight loss with disapproval, and the next time Jennifer visited him, a scale sat in the middle of his office. The shiny rectangle on the floor seemed so out of place among the more formal furniture in the room, a symbol of failure that may as well have screamed at her, mocking her inability to maintain control over something as simple as food.

You can't handle this. The thought pelted her brain.

The number flashed up like a neon sign: In trying to lose six pounds, she'd lost nineteen. And she wasn't done.

*****

Jennifer didn't—couldn't—see the difference in the mirror. She did notice other changes, though. Her thick hair was falling out. It wasn't really noticeable to anyone else because she had so much of it, but Jen saw the clumps of it in her hand after she ran her fingers through the strands. Her belly, now flat (concave, really), was covered in a downy fur that hadn't been there before. Jen thought of it as her own personal peach fuzz.

Her hair and body weren't the only things affected by her refusal to nourish herself. Jennifer found it harder and harder to focus. Her brain was running on empty, and it became difficult to remember things. Daydreaming —never an issue for her before—happened daily.

"... and she asked us whether we wanted to chip in on a gift. What do you think?" Marc asked.

Jennifer paused before responding, desperately trying to backtrack to the last thing she could remember them discussing. "Um ... sure," she said, slowly hoping that was the right answer.

"Do you even know what I just said?" Marc asked, the frustration very clear in his voice.

"Sorry, babe. I zoned out for a bit," Jen said, sheepishly.

"What else is new?" he tried to joke but both knew it wasn't funny in the least.

*****

Her energy level was zilch. Some days she had to will herself to get up, the effort to simply leave her bed seeming monumental. But she still managed to exercise, pushing herself to ride her requisite daily 13 miles in the blistering summer sun. She'd added crunches to the mix: hundreds each day that added up to thousands, each more punishing then the last.

Dr. Dorian was stern and plain spoken, pushing her to eat. He wanted to refer her to an eating disorder specialist at Johns Hopkins University. Jennifer refused, telling him they didn't take her insurance, telling herself she didn't want to change. Secretly, she *did* want to feel better mentally and emotionally, but she was happy about being thinner and didn't want that part to change. Jennifer couldn't see that it was all connected. Her lack of energy, loss of focus, and forgetfulness were all the result of her refusal to eat.

The number on the scale continued to drop.

*****

Somewhere along the way, purging became part of her weight loss plan. She was surprised at how easy it was to make herself throw up what she'd just eaten. A finger down her throat, a small tickle, and out would come the hateful food that threatened to make her gain weight. Unlike many who purge, Jennifer was not a binge eater—purging was not a way to undo the damage of overeating. Instead, it was just a result of having food in her stomach that gave her any sense of being full. Even a bowl of cereal could prove uncomfortable, but a quick trip to the bathroom could remedy that.

Marc's concerns grew. He knew about the purging, which would sometimes happen at a restaurant just after a meal. She'd excuse herself from the table to go to the restroom, and he'd watch her walk away, sadly knowing what she was about to do. Powerless to stop her but afraid to upset her, he'd raise the topic without confrontation. Knowing his wife the way he did, he sensed that if he pushed too hard she'd simply dig her heels in. Instead, he tried negotiating.

"You don't have to eat that, but will you at least try half of this?" he'd probe. Or, "Where can we go to eat that has something on the menu you'll be okay with?" he'd say, hoping she'd allow herself to indulge in something that had some substance, but knowing full well she wouldn't.

The negotiations failed. Jennifer kept dropping weight. Dr. Dorian played hardball, threatening to force her into the hospital if she lost any more. Marc asked, then pleaded with, her to get help.

Her therapist Jackie tried too, cajoling her in a less confrontational way to consider hospitalization as a way to get better. "You know, you're going through some pretty big stuff right now. And that's bound to feel like a heavy burden. But you don't have to go through it alone. What if they could make it easier for you? It doesn't have to be so overwhelming, you know. Will you at least think about it?"

Jackie had touched on an important point. It would be nice to be around others who understood what it was like to battle their own body.

Jennifer agreed. Something inside her knew that she had to. She was afraid of losing everything. She knew she needed help, and she was ready to accept it. She'd do it for Marc. For their marriage. Jennifer checked herself into Shephard Pratt Health System in Towson, Maryland. It would be the first of three times she'd be hospitalized for Anorexia Nervosa.

*****

Marc sat next to her in the empty reception area as Jennifer filled out form after form. Each piece of stark white paper demanded details, the information that was intended to show who she was as a person. Inside, Jennifer resisted: the form knew nothing. Nothing she could write on it would capture why she was starving herself. She gave the know-nothing forms to the receptionist and was led down the brightly lit hall to weigh in.

The scale showed just how far Jennifer had punished herself: 104.

She went into the hospital that first time expecting it to be a short stay. She'd do what they asked of her just to get everyone off her back. And when she was done, she could go home and continue to do exactly what she'd been doing.

Her 'short stay' ended up with her being in-patient for three weeks, with a partial hospitalization for six more. Unending days of appointments with doctors and staff members. And therapy. Every kind she could think of: Individual. Group. Family. There were sessions with nutritionists. Meal times. And weighing in every day.

Of course, that part was nothing new. Jennifer had been weighing herself every day for years. What was new was only weighing in *once* a day. She was used to 10-12 times a day, everyday. When she got out of bed. Before and after eating. Before and after purging. Before and after going to the bathroom, and exercising, and any other time it occurred to her. That she would only step on a scale once a day was odd and unsettling but that one weight determined how her day in the hospital would go: if she didn't hit the weight goal that had been set for her that day, she lost privileges.

Those privileges were everything for someone who felt trapped.

If she didn't make weight, she couldn't make phone calls. Showers were not allowed. Neither were visitors. Outside was off limits. It all hinged on that damned scale.

And it wasn't as though they weren't stuffing her full of food in an attempt to help her gain back some substance. The staff eased her into it, of course. When the body's been deprived of nutrients for so long, it's important to keep the electrolytes in check. Jen got very small portions for the first few days, but ate more frequently. As her body adjusted, the amounts of food increased. Soon she was eating three times a day plus two snacks. It was overwhelming for her. Disheartening. And she felt disgusting.

Jennifer felt her control slipping away.

*****

PLEASE

Please don't leave me here;
Inside myself.
Don't go away and leave me alone.
Pull me out,
Out of the rubble.
Take me with you.

It's lonely here
In this place;
I don't know where I am.
Would you stay, if I was good?
Could you leave me then?

Please don't walk away,
Shut me out, push me further into my hell.
I'll drown here,
You would too.
Please hold me, don't let go.
Would you hold me if I was pretty?

Please don't give up on me.
I've done it to myself already.

Don't ignore me, pretending I'm not me.
Would you pay attention to me if I was healthy?

Would you stop and turn around?
Glancing back,
Making sure I am okay.
Would you? Please do.
Please let me come too.

*****

The first time Marc came to visit, they sat in the cafeteria. Bright overhead fixtures highlighted the marks in the long, wooden tables where patients had used their utensils to carve initials and other symbols meaningful only to them. The pair sat next to each other, holding hands, as they talked about Jen's experiences so far.

"The food sucks."

"Not as good as my Hamburger Helper?" Marc joked.

"I'm not kidding! And God, there's so much and they make me eat it all. I feel like I'm going to explode."

Marc traced one of the tabletop carvings with his free hand, the tactile action soothing him. "How are the other patients? Have you met anyone you connect with?"

"A couple of people, I guess. I still feel out of place, though. I just wanna come home."

Marc knew furthering the conversation would be useless at that point. She wasn't ready to leave and they both knew it. He'd brought a deck of Skip Bo cards with him and pulled them out of his pocket, hoping to distract her. It worked. The two played cards for the rest of the visit, Jen winning every hand as Marc grumbled about her streak of luck. If the setting had been different, an onlooker never would've known the stresses these two, and their marriage, were facing.

*****

THAT Girl

Do you see her smile?
Do you hear her laugh?
Can you smell the light scent of freshly cut grass in her hair?
Who is THAT girl?
Watch her; watch her twirl and jump.
Watch when she trips but doesn't fall.
THAT girl; was it me?
Was i THAT girl,
That happy girl?

Look as she dances,
She doesn't know you're there.
THAT girl is alone in her world.
Not lonely.
It's a happy place; peaceful.
Do you know her?
Have you ever seen her here?

When did she fade away?
Where did she hide?
Where did her smile go?
Bright eyes replaced with sunken valleys.
Cries of laughter, now cries of pain.
If you squint, can you see her?
Can you see THAT girl?

*****

It's difficult to see yourself as others do, and Jennifer learned that during her stay in Sheppard Pratt. Before she arrived, she just *knew* she'd be the heaviest person there. And when she got there, she looked around at all the other patients, noticing how stick-thin they were and thinking how incredibly sick they looked. *Good thing I don't look like they do,* Jennifer thought. *They really need help.*

But Jen had a false sense of security. She still *felt* overweight despite the scale clocking her in at just over 100 pounds. During lunch (which only lasted an hour—too little time to stretch out the food to make her stay fuller, longer), Jen sat with Catherine, a patient she'd befriended. The two of them watched Sarah stroll across the hall. Sarah was tall and blonde, and very, very, *very* thin.

"Do you know the staff keeps confusing us?" Jennifer told Catherine. "They're so stupid. I can't figure out why they can't tell us apart. We don't look anything alike!"

"Yeah, you do," came Catherine's reply. "I can totally see it."

"But she's so much skinnier than I am!" Jennifer argued. Catherine looked at her like she had eight heads. "No, she's not, Jen. She's really not."

Jennifer didn't see it, nor did she believe her friend. She still felt fat.

*****

While Jennifer and Marc definitely needed therapy to work through their situation, family therapy at Sheppard Pratt was not geared toward solving a couple's problems. Instead, it was designed to help them function together to address Jen's needs both during hospitalization and at home afterwards, offering the best chances at recovery. The counselor would address issues like eating disorder triggers, things Marc should watch for so that he didn't inadvertently say or do something that would undo Jennifer's progress. It was an important teaching tool, but it didn't come close to helping them get to the bottom of their own situation.

*****

Jen's parents came to visit a few times. Awkward and stilted conversation made it nearly unbearable.

"Well, his beard has come in nicely," Cindy said about Marc after he left the room to bring them all bottles of water. It was his way of escaping the tension for a few minutes; it was Cindy's way of acknowledging his transition. Jen had talked with her mom about using the right pronouns, and Cindy was making the effort to correct it.

Despite her mother's attempt, Jen was not in the mood to congratulate her mom. "Yep," was all she managed.

Idle chit-chat filled the rest of the visit, as though Jen were at home instead of a psychiatric facility. Everyone pretended all was fine.

In a way, it reminded Jen of the numerous times she'd tried unsuccessfully to console her mom during a depressive episode. It was a pattern for them—Cindy, in tears and overwrought while Jennifer did her best to comfort her mother and help her feel better. One time in particular, Jen recalled sitting on the floor at the end of the bed as her mother wept. Staring at the floral wallpaper, she chastised herself. She'd tried so hard to help and was tired of trying. Tired of failing. Defeated again, this time she'd given up. Instead of rubbing her mom's back or holding her hand to offer sympathy, she sat on the floor and listened to her mother weeping. Eventually, Jennifer became determined to block out her own emotions. She taught herself to keep from crying or getting angry. She learned to pretend everything was fine. And here they all were, dealing with the repercussions of that.

*****

Over the years, Jennifer had performed in a few community theatre productions, enjoying the chance to dance again and scoring several acting roles, as well. She found herself using those acting skills to convince the staff at Sheppard Pratt she was well enough to go home. At last the scale cooperated and she was discharged—free to leave and care for herself.

She'd never known such a feeling of freedom as she did walking out of the hospital that day. Somehow the sun seemed brighter, the air was sweeter, her world more comforting. She luxuriated in the love of her pets, the cat rubbing against her ankle and Tinkerbell, her tiny dog, jumping up and down with joy. She welcomed with a sigh the feeling of being back in her own bed, her husband beside her.

Jennifer returned to her job at the cardiologists' office, glad to be back. Life was as it should be, her stint in the hospital just a bad dream that derailed her from her life. She craved her normal routine and eagerly sank right back into it: work, workouts, and all. Old habits die hard, as they say, and Jen took comfort in once again taking control over how, and how much, she ate.

She found new ways to keep her calorie intake down. She'd skip breakfast entirely, striving to make it to lunch before she put anything in her body. One p.m. became her new goal. If she held out that long, she could keep her numbers down for the day, eating less and losing the weight they'd made her gain at the hospital.

Jen also set a new calorie goal for herself: 600 calories a day. Her time at Shephard Pratt had changed nothing. Not only was she no better off mentally than when she went in, she was too sick physically to change anything about it.

This period of time—this obsession with her body, her weight, herself—was good for one thing: it allowed her to block out Marc and everything to do with transitions, hormones, and anything else going on in her life. She didn't have to pretend it wasn't there; she didn't have the mental capacity to even think about it. Her brain, operating at such a deficit because of her diet, wouldn't allow it. She only had enough energy to obsess about food.

*****

"Jen, may I speak with you please." Lydia issued an order, not a question. Jennifer had been out of the hospital and back at work for exactly one week.

"Sure." Dread filled her instantly. Lydia's prepared speech was totally unnecessary. Jen knew what she was going to say before she said it.

"I'm afraid we're going to have to let you go. Your ... situation ... is affecting the office. I can't have co-workers distracted by what is happening to you personally. I have a check here for two weeks' salary."

Jennifer took it wordlessly. She was defeated. Embarrassed. And too sick to care too much.

*****

It took just two weeks before Jennifer found herself back at the hospital again. Filling out the same ridiculous, know-nothing forms. Meeting the same stupid doctors and therapists. Greeting the familiar patients that either hadn't left yet or had already checked back in like her. Sarah was still there. So was Catherine. Nothing had changed.

It was déjà vu.

＊＊＊＊＊

Tomorrow

I only hate today,
What tomorrow will be worse.
This life that was so beautiful has now become a curse.

I curse the day that I was born,
Into this life i hate.
i curse the day that i will die
A disappointment i will make.

I never thought i'd live this long,
To suffer every day.
i thought that i would long be gone;
down with my life i lay.

I curse the moments of happiness
For they are only a nasty trick.
I curse love and life and beauty
That make my mind so sick.

＊＊＊＊＊

Meal times at the hospital sucked. They forced her to eat what felt like an enormous amount of food, and every bite was strictly monitored in the sterile, institutionalized cafeteria. The staff was well versed in every trick that patients use to get away with not eating. They knew patients would wear baggy socks to hide food when no one was looking. They watched for the napkin trick—a patient pretending to wipe their mouth, but actually spitting food into the napkin instead. Food that was "accidentally" dropped on the floor to avoid being eaten would be replaced immediately.

She had to eat everything, every morsel. Staff members watched as Jennifer ate, making sure she didn't cut up her food in pieces that were too small, a sure sign that she'd try to hide the food. She wasn't allowed to wear more than one layer of clothing so she couldn't smuggle any food out instead of eating it. After mealtime was over, they'd make her turn out her pockets and take off her shoes to be sure she hadn't hidden any food in them.

There was a standard meal plan. Jennifer could choose from among several options, but she had to finish every bite on her plate. Choices included everything from sandwiches to a turkey dinner, each seeming more repellent than the last. She got nauseated just making her selections, thinking of the shameful and offensive calories each would contain, every one of those little suckers looking to undo all of her hard work.

Jen couldn't believe how much they made her eat! Even if she ate it all, she didn't always gain, and if she didn't make weight for the day, they'd increase the amount she had to eat for the next day. And if she *still* didn't make weight, she was put on the "tall menu" because of her height, which meant she was served double the amount of protein. Forcing herself to eat double the food, Jennifer felt heinous and overfull. That wasn't the worst of it though. When she still missed her weight after being on the tall menu, they added Ensure Plus, a nutritional supplement, to increase her caloric intake. Then they added two. Then three. Eventually, she was up to the maximum amount per day—four Ensures, laden with vile calories that threatened to make her gain weight. Three meals, two snacks, and four Ensures each day. It was revolting.

But she did it. She did what she was asked. But only for those two weeks, because her insurance wouldn't cover the costs for her to stay any longer. She was once again free ... free to leave and do as she pleased.

*****

i know what it's like

i know what it's like to want to die.
To want to bleed out a life;
a life of pain, and strife;
a life not worth living.

i know what it's like to wish for death
in sleeplessness and wakelessness;
an escape from the struggle,

the background noise of your own head.

i know what it's like to hope you'll sleep;
a sleep so deep you won't wake up.
A peaceful sleep, no cares, no dreams.

i know what it's like to be broken down
without a hope to live or die;
so numb, so emotionally void.

i know what it's like to pray for courage;
the courage to push the blade in further,
the courage to swallow one more pill.

i know what it's like not to care.
Not to think, or feel, or want to try.

i know what it's like to lose yourself
in life, in love, in my own reflection.

i know what it's like to wake up crying,
sorting out dream from memory;
not knowing what's real.

i know what it's like to feel alone.
Lonely, solitary, confined to my own mind.

i know what it's like to be afraid;
of living, of dying, of just being me.

******

This time, Jennifer managed to stay out of the hospital for a while. She was trying to get better; she really was. She knew if she continued her behavior, she wouldn't be able to function. Anorexia has a startlingly high mortality rate, but Jen never saw her disease as life threatening. That didn't mean she didn't think about what it would be like to die. To just lie there and not get out of bed. *I can't do this anymore*, she thought more than once. *I'm just too tired.*

Jen made half-hearted attempts to eat, to get better. She tried to eat a little more, to cut back on the exercising. It was too little, too late. Her body simply didn't have the strength, and she didn't have the mental energy to push herself to do any more than she was doing.

So she returned to the hospital again. *Third time's the charm*, she thought.

*****

Ugly Girl

Do you see her?
Do you see that ugly girl;
Do you see how sad she's gotten?
Do you see how sick she's become?

I see her growing sadder;
I see her wrapped in pain.
I see the guilt that shrouds her;
I don't even know her name.

Do you know that person?
Do you weep for her;
Or do you turn and walk away,
Thinking that you're better?

Try to look closer.
Try to feel her pain,
Try to look inside yourself,
And see if you're to blame.

I see her drifting slowly
From this darkened place.
I see her drowning in her sorrow,
She has sacrificed this race.

It's like a different person.
Someone I don't know.
Some reckless force of nature,

Begging her not to grow.

The force, it grows much stronger;
And that girl is weak.
She can't hold on much longer,
That girl can't see or speak.

She lost her voice to those louder;
Louder and stronger than she.
She lost her sight to those who pass by,
And refuse to stop and weep.

Weep for the girl that's gone,
And the fragile body still
Clinging to a precipice
With so little strength and will.

When you watch her slipping,
Do you care for her enough?
To grab her hand and hold it,
To put aside your stuff.

*****

When she went back to the hospital this time, she'd been gone long enough it really was like starting all over. New doctors, new therapists, new counselors and nutritionists. *Great. Starting my life story all over again,* she thought. *These damned forms! Does anyone even ever* read *them?* At least some of the patients were familiar, sad to say. Jen recognized a few of them from her previous stays. It provided little comfort.

She was assigned to a doctor she hadn't met before. She was a pretty woman, but Jennifer couldn't stand her. Not because she wasn't a good doctor—she probably was great. But she always had lipstick on her teeth. Jen couldn't stop staring at it. She requested a new physician.

Something about this stay was different. Not only did Jennifer feel like she'd hit bottom during her time at home, but she was tired. Tired of fighting. Tired of feeling like crap. Tired of being tired. She was ready to get well.

She found irony in the idea that she could accept the changes in her husband's body easier than she could her own. Jennifer worked on self-acceptance, trying to love herself as she was and not as she thought she *should* be. She *could* handle it, she told herself. *My mom was wrong.*

She was also closer to her goal weight when she entered the hospital this time, too, which helped make the journey slightly easier to take this time; the more reasonable number seemed less daunting. Her team of physicians set a new goal weight, and Jen resolved to achieve it. *If I can get to that weight and it doesn't kill me, maybe I can live with it. Maybe there is life after this disease.* Because she actually saw it as a sickness now. Something had changed. *She* had changed.

*****

(untitled)

overflowing with sadness,
but not knowing why.
My ship is sinking,
floods of tears.
Black like night
no stars, no moonlight.
Dark behind my eyes.
nothingness…
Where is this god you talk of?
no trust, no faith.
Dig deep to find your strength,
but nothing's there but darkness,
a black hole.
Who wants to see that?
Don't look too hard,
don't ask
and I won't tell.
I'll stand lonely in my darkness
You stay happy in your light.

Waiting in the dark.
someone…set me free!

curled up and losing air;
pull me to the surface, please.

A voice speaks from deep within,
barely recognizable.
One that hasn't been heard in such a long time
it's faint, but clear.

"Swim up little one, don't stay down here.
Swim up to the light and set yourself free.
You're stronger than you know.
The ones you love are waiting at the top.
Swim up little one, you have miles to go,
but don't stop. Don't hide down here,
you'll never be free. You'll suffocate down here,
you can't hear or see.
Swim up, swim up, swim up little one."

It's time to decide.
Which way will I choose?
Staying down here would be easy, but there would be no peace.
I'd stay here tormented by my thoughts in my sleep.
If I choose to swim up, the path will be hard;
long, dark and lonely, but there would be a reward.
I'd find myself there, on the top, in the light.
No more darkness surrounding me; no more demons in sight.

*****

It took her six weeks to get there, but Jennifer actually worked hard to succeed this time. When she stepped on the hospital scale and saw that number, she knew she could make it.

Coming home was different too. Marc policed her now, forcing her to eat whether she wanted to or not. So she did.

It'd been a little over two years since Jennifer first made her New Year's resolution to lose six pounds. In that time, she'd lost more than weight. She'd lost her way. Her sense of self. And for a time, her sanity. But her marriage was still intact, her husband by her side, and for the first time in more than two years, Jennifer felt they were ready to face the future— together.

*****

One Chance

What if you only got one chance?
One chance in a lifetime.
No mistakes, errors, flaws, or mishaps.
What if that was it?
You were finished, done, dead,
With one missed step.

Why do I live like this?
Why do I punish myself for every mistake;
Every flaw?
There will always be another chance;
Another day, another try.
Why do I pick up where the universe leaves off?
How did I become so driven,
So frightened I might not be perfect?

I will always have another chance to make things right.
There will be another tomorrow.
Today will become yesterday, the past.

It will all be in the past.
Do I spend the rest of my life regretting the past,
Or do I take another chance;
Another step, another try, another risk?

One chance is not enough.
We would all lose the game.

Striving for perfection, and
Falling short makes life limited.
Striving for happiness, for love,
For one more chance, for another day,
Another tomorrow.

Chapter 11
Who are We?

"So, feel like tying the knot today?"

"I do," Jen joked.

After being married for four years, this was the day that they'd officially be wed in the eyes of the court. It was a beautiful September day, and the pair had a date at the courthouse in Washington, D.C., where same-sex marriage was legal. It was more than a gesture—being recognized as man and wife was important to them in multiple ways.

Health insurance was fortunately not a concern. Jen had landed a new job, and Marc was still at the radio station; both employers covered their healthcare.

However, tax benefits were definitely improved by filing jointly, which they weren't able to do up until now.

Jennifer also wanted to take Marc's name. Jennifer Taylor was ready to be recognized by the world as Mrs. Marc Wyndham.

But the most compelling reason had nothing to with paying the government less money or changing a name. It had to do with their legal rights.

When they had their wedding ceremony in Maryland in 2006, same-sex marriage wasn't legal so their union wasn't recognized in the eyes of the law. Given Jen's recent mental health issues, both were concerned that someone could fight to intervene on Jen's behalf and Marc might not have the legal recourse that is afforded a spouse. Hence, the plan for today: a simple ceremony that would make their marriage bound by the courts instead of only by their hearts.

*****

The weather cooperated just as it had the first time they said, "I do." It was a beautiful late summer day in the nation's Capital as Jennifer and Marc entered the courthouse.

Wood paneled and austere, the room where marriage ceremonies were performed definitely felt like a courtroom—with one noticeable exception.

"What is *that*?" Jen asked softly so only Marc could hear.

"They must pull that out for the celebrity weddings," he laughed.

It was a trellis with fake vines and plastic flowers obviously meant to soften the business-like feel of the room. It was the only spot of white in the otherwise stark chamber, and it stood out like a sore thumb. As tacky as it was tasteless, Jen and Marc both knew it would be one of things they'd remember about the day.

"Everyone here?" the officiant asked. Her voice was warm, welcoming. The couple nodded and offered up their paperwork, filled out a month before in anticipation of today. "Hi, I'm Liz. It's a pleasure to meet you."

Jen shook hands first. "Nice to meet you too. I'm Jennifer and this is my husband, Marc. Well, almost my husband." Everyone laughed, and Liz asked if there were any witnesses they'd like to be present.

"Nope, just us," Marc answered.

"Then let's get started."

The ceremony was simple. The couple hadn't written vows or worried about extra verbiage—this wasn't about being flowery, it was about being legal. A short ten minutes later, it was done. They were officially husband and wife, still sharing their lives together but now also sharing a name and the security that their rights were protected by law.

******

Walking the two blocks to the Metro station to catch the train back out of town, Jen felt lighter. She took her husband's hand.

"I know it's just a piece of paper, but I feel different, don't you?"

"Yeah, I do," Marc agreed. "I just like knowing it's legal. Like no matter what happens, we're official."

They boarded the Metro train and sat. Jen noticed a young black man do a double-take when he saw them.

"Do you know him?" She indicated the man with a slight move of her head. Marc looked over.

"Doesn't look familiar," Marc said. Just then, the guy left his seat to come toward the couple.

"Yo, you the guy from YouTube?" the man asked. "I've seen you!"

Marc looked up in amazement. "Uh, yeah, that's me!"

Marc's YouTube videos had been a way to show his loved ones the testosterone-driven developments in his body. He hadn't necessarily thought about strangers watching his progression from Marika to Marc. Not that he minded—he simply hadn't expected to be recognized by someone in public.

"Dude, I'm really glad you posted those videos!" He introduced himself. "Sorry. I'm Mo. Used to be Maureen."

"Hey, good to meet you!" Marc shook his hand and introduced Mo to Jennifer.

"I started to transition two years ago, and I watched everything I could find so I'd know what to expect. That's how I saw you. I can't believe I'm meeting you!"

"I'm glad they helped." Marc wasn't really sure what else to say. It was kind of fun to be recognized but here was a total stranger he knew nothing about. "You look great," he added, awkwardly.

Mo, sensing that Marc seemed to be self-conscious, backed off. "Thanks. And thanks again for those videos." He shook his head to himself as he headed back to his seat. "Can't believe I met him," he said to himself as he walked away.

Marc grinned at his wife. "See? Told you that trellis thing was for celebrity weddings."

Jen smiled back. She knew how uncomfortable he could feel sometimes, and she was proud of how he'd handled the strange encounter. More importantly, she was proud he was her husband.

The train slowed for the next stop.

Chapter 12
Lost and Found

Jen reached over and turned out the light. Dark, quiet, only the room seemed to breathe while she held her breath. Somewhat awkwardly, she reached out to touch Marc. Meaning to caress his arm, she extended her arm farther than she'd intended and brushed his nipple instead. He startled and jerked away.

"Sorry." Stung, Jen pulled her arm away.

Marc realized he'd hurt her and rolled on his side to face his wife. "Babe..." he started, but Jennifer wasn't having it.

"It's okay. Never mind."

Both rolled away from each other, eyes wide open, sleep the last thing on either of their minds.

*****

This awkwardness in bed was their new normal. And it was to be expected, the therapists said, but that didn't make it any easier to manage or less hurtful for either of them. Jen felt like she didn't know what Marc wanted, and the ironic thing was, neither did Marc. They were like two familiar strangers, trying to learn what the other wanted but feeling they should already know the answer. And because at one time, they *had* known, it made them all the more uncomfortable with each other.

Of course, that was true outside of the bedroom too. They could be sitting the in the same room together and feel like the Grand Canyon was between them. It wasn't that they weren't getting along; on the contrary, they were both making every effort to be kind. But neither wanted to upset the other, so they danced around potentially painful discussions like two professional ballerinas, tiptoeing past the pitfalls with smiles on their faces. It was only a matter of time before they fell headlong into them.

*****

"Babe, wanna go see Avatar tonight?" Marc was dying to see the movie he'd heard so much about. More than that, he was trying desperately to get his wife out of the house. She'd been in a funk for a few months, and he didn't know how to reach her. Withdrawn and depressed, her emotional state was exhausting for both of them.

Her sadness seemed to be limitless. He'd tried everything he could think of to bring her out of it; he'd been sympathetic, he'd offered support, he'd planned a surprise weekend away. No matter what he did, it seemed she'd never again feel anything but hopeless.

The depression this time was likely caused by antidepressant withdrawal. Jennifer had taken herself off of the drugs because they'd left her feeling numb, zombie-like with no emotions at all. The nightmares they'd caused were the worst. Terrifyingly black, they left her exhausted. Jennifer decided she'd rather cope with depression then deal with the side effects of the Effexor and Abilify she'd been prescribed. She didn't talk about it with her doctor; she simply made the decision to stop cold turkey, and her body (and her mental health) reeled in response.

Jen couldn't even respond to Marc's question about the movie. She just shook her head, still in bed. It was three in the afternoon.

"Come on, you gotta try," Marc pleaded.

"I can't."

"God, Jen, I don't know how much more of this I can take! If you can't even make the effort..." He stormed from the room.

I can't make the effort, she thought. *I don't care enough to try.*

*****

Are You Afraid of the Dark?

Are you afraid of the dark?
So afraid of the darkness that you live in the gray?
Afraid to come into the light; afraid the shadows will bite?
So afraid that the light will fade,
So scared that there's always a trade.
There's not light without darkness.
You can have both or none.
You can't have the moon if there were no sun.

Do you choose the gray, because it's easy to stay?
Out of fear, you remain,
Stuck in the gloom, in the haze.
I've lived in the darkness, and danced in the light.
Escaping the dark is an ongoing fight.
The light's just as scary because it may end.
So I'll try the gray, its safe haven; a friend.
But friends can be fickle and sometimes they fool.
The gray can be lonely, so foggy, and cool.
But the light is too risky, I remain on the edge.
Hoping, waiting, still trying to conquer this ledge.
It's a fence of decision, and I don't dare decide,
In the gray I won't face it, I may need to hide.
The darkness comes calling at least once a day,
The light is so tempting to carry me away,
But I'll not answer either, it's here I will stay
So lonely, so desperate, just me in the gray.

*****

Marc's comment washed over Jen again and again. *I don't know how much more of this I can take. I don't know how much more of this I can take.*

A thought crossed her mind for the first time. What if he gave up? What if he was through trying? Where would she be without him? All of this time, she'd felt that she could decide whether their marriage survived. Suddenly, she realized he also had a say. This, too, could be out of her control.

The thought of losing him was terrifying. He was her world. She'd gone through so much—*they'd* gone through so much—he couldn't just leave now. Where would that leave her?

The panic attack hit without warning. Jen sat up quickly, thoughts churning uncontrollably. *He can't leave! He can't leave!* Spiraling like a dervish, her thoughts wound tighter and tighter, almost strangling her brain. Heart pounding, Jen couldn't catch her breath. She made her way to the bathroom, sure she would vomit.

Once there, neither the nauseous feeling nor the anxiety abated. Jen struggled to breathe, hoping to force her chest into allowing a lungful of air. Her head dropped as she gave herself over to the full brunt of the attack.

Sweating palms, tingling fingers, she nearly itched with the intensity of her emotions. She glanced over to the sink where the scissors caught her eye and they were in her hand in an instant, poised to descend.

*****

Marc quietly opened the door, hoping he'd find Jennifer awake but trying not to disturb her if she'd fallen asleep. Seeing the empty bed, he turned toward the bathroom. The too-familiar scene flashed before him and he knew what she'd done.

"Oh God, honey! No!" He rushed in to see how much damage she'd done.

"It's okay, it's not that bad, I'm okay." Jen was breathing easier. The panic attack sated, she was in the sweet oblivion that always followed her cutting.

"I'm gonna call the doctor." Marc handed her a towel and kissed the top of her head, torn between wanting to be next to her and knowing he needed to leave to get her help. His heart dropped as he realized he once again was powerless to help his wife.

*****

"She either starts back on those meds tonight or you've got to get her to the hospital." The doctor's voice was firm. He was frustrated. Marc had told him she'd taken herself off the drugs, which was not only foolish but medically dangerous. "I mean it. Either find a 24-hour pharmacy and get those prescriptions filled, or take her to the ER."

Marc went to plead with his wife.

*****

"I'm not taking them. No!" Jennifer was nothing if not stubborn. "If you wanna take me to the hospital, fine. But I'm not taking them."

Miserable, Marc buttoned Jen's coat as she held the towel against her wounds. The pair headed for the car.

*****

They lucked out; it was a quiet night at the ER, and they were seen right away. Jen felt almost like she had the flu: achy, weak and spent, she sat quietly as Marc filled the doctor in on what had happened and his conversation with Jen's psychiatrist.

"Now that you're here, how about taking the meds so we can get you feeling better?" the ER doctor asked.

"Nope."

"I wish you'd reconsider. But if you won't take them, I can give you some Attivan to help you relax, at least."

The euphoria she felt from her earlier cutting had already dissipated. Concerned about another panic attack, she acquiesced. "Okay," she said.

*****

The nurse came in and handed Jen a medicine cup, one small white Lorazepam its only contents. As she turned her back to pour water into a cup, Jennifer noticed the purple scrubs she wore bore images of tiny calico cats chasing balls of string.

"This should make you feel better," she said, handing the water to Jen.

She swallowed the pill as the doctor walked in, the water cool as it washed down her throat.

"So, I just need you to sign this, and we can let you go." He offered her a piece of paper and sure enough, it was the same form she'd been given before.

"Nope."

"What?" he said, sure she didn't understand what he'd just handed her. "This is just a form for us to release you. You just need to sign it so we can send you home."

"I'm not signing," Jen said, stubbornly.

"Can I ask why?" The doctor failed to understand why Jen would refuse. It likely seemed so simple to him.

"Cuz I don't want to." Jen's reply was as petulant as the expression on her face, daring him to make her do something she didn't want to.

"If you won't sign it, you'll have to stay here," the doctor said.

"I'm not signing it, and I'm not staying."

The doctor wasn't sure what to do. He'd never had someone refuse to sign before. "I'll be back," he said, before leaving to ask someone else how to handle this. Jen could almost imagine him scratching his head at her behavior as he left.

Marc watched the scene unfold, not sure what to make of his wife's actions.

"What's going on, babe?" Marc asked.

"I don't want to sign the damn form, that's what." Jen said, exasperated.

"Why? Don't you want to go home?" Marc questioned.

"I'm tired of being told what to do."

Exasperated and exhausted, Marc let that go. They waited for the doctor.

*****

"So, I've talked with someone from our psych department, and I'm afraid we're going to have to admit you."

"What? No." Jennifer was emphatic. This was nonsense.

"There are two ways this can happen." The doctor was as determined as Jennifer. "You can voluntarily check yourself in, or we'll admit you against your will."

"Okay, fine, I'll sign the damn thing," Jen said.

"I'm sorry. It's too late for that," The doctor said, every bit as resolute as Jennifer had been just minutes before.

"No, I changed my mind. I'll sign. Just give it to me so I can get out of here," Jen pleaded.

"I can't let you do that."

"But I just want to go home."

Marc stepped in, trying to help. "Babe, maybe it's better for you to check in. Just say you want to stay." He knew she needed to be here. She was beyond any help he could give her at home.

Jennifer was confused. Why was Marc also ganging up on her? Why were they all against her?

"Fine." Resigned and heartsick, she checked herself in to the hospital.

*****

Oh God, not you. Jennifer couldn't believe her bad luck. The psychiatrist on call that night was one she'd seen briefly in college, when she'd experienced a brief bout of depression. This guy was about as sensitive as a stick.

"I hear you won't take your medicine." His thick Indian accent did nothing to give him an air of concern. He was unfeeling, uncaring, and ineffective. Or at least that's how Jen remembered him. *He has as little compassion as he does hair*, she thought.

"Nope." Pushed, Jen held firm on her position.

"You have to take the medicine or you won't feel any better," the doctor said.

"I'm not taking it."

"Well, then I'm afraid there is nothing I can do for you." And with that he walked out of the room, refusing to talk to her.

*****

The doctor tried again the next morning.

"How are you feeling today?" he asked.

"The same," she responded.

"Will you take your medicine now?" the doctor tried again.

"Nope," she said.

"Then I am wasting my time here. Maybe tomorrow you'll change your mind," and out he went, leaving Jennifer to face a long, lonely day in the hospital room.

*****

The following morning, the same doctor offered a choice after Jen refused, again, to take the medicines everyone but her seemed to feel she needed.

"Would you like some Prozac?" he asked.

Jen quickly agreed, knowing that at least it would be something to take the edge off. But as long as she refused to take the Effexor and Abilify, the doctor would have nothing else to do with her. She was on her own.

*****

After four days of getting nowhere, it was time to force action. A meeting was called at the hospital—an intervention of sorts. They gathered in the psych unit's conference room. Jennifer, Marc, Jen's parents, and a social worker sat around a fiberboard table, the wood laminate finish chipping around the edges. Vinyl chairs groaned as everyone settled in to them. Tense and terse, they'd all come together to figure out what to do about Jennifer.

"We seem to be in a stalemate here," said the social worker, who'd introduced herself as Pam. "Jennifer doesn't want to take her medicines, and we can't keep her here indefinitely. So, I think we need to figure out what our next steps are."

"You could just let me go." The answer seemed so simple to Jen.

"We could, but I'm afraid that you'd just end up right back here if we did. Something needs to change."

"She can come home with us," Cindy said, helpfully. "Maybe she needs a break. Maybe a chance to think things through would help her?" Jen thought she sensed her mother's tone change from helpful to hopeful. *Yeah, you'd really like that, wouldn't you?* she thought. *You'd get your way. I'd be home.*

"That's not a bad idea," Marc said. Jennifer was shocked that he would agree. Seeing the surprise on her face, he continued. "Of course I want you home, babe. But I don't know how to help you. Maybe a change of scenery would be good."

She felt defeated. Deflated. And so alone. Marc turned to her, grabbing her hands. "I love you. I want you to get better. I just don't know how to help you do that. I think this might be good for you."

And almost as an afterthought, he added, "For us."

*****

The stay with her parents lasted three weeks, and Jen did her best to cope with a situation over which she had no power. She went back on her medications, begrudgingly, finally accepting that the status quo was certainly not working. She went to the office as much as she could. She was working as a technician for a retinal surgeon now, and she dragged herself to the surgical center, craving the routine it provided as much as the escape from her mother's ever-watchful eye. Still, she often found she couldn't force herself out of bed, instead cocooning herself in blackness to block out all emotion. The nightmares that had plagued her when she was on the meds before returned, but she at least welcomed the gray oblivion of sleep that shrouded her in nothingness in between the haunted dreams. It was better than the never-ending sadness that had beset her once she stopped taking the drugs.

Cindy tried to take care of her as much as Jen would allow it. And Jennifer tried to let her. But in her mind, the care came with a price.

"Would you like me to make you some soup?" her mom offered one afternoon. It was a dreary, late-winter day in March, and the temperature was as low as Jen's spirits.

"Yeah, sounds good, Mom. Thanks."

But with the chicken noodle came penance when Cindy entered the bedroom and set the tray beside Jennifer on the bed. "How are you feeling? Do you think it's helping, you having a bit of space?"

Jen sensed where the conversation was headed faster than a GPS could recalculate.

"Mom, thanks for the soup, but I think I'm going to try to rest now." She shut things down before they could go any further. In her mind, this was punishment. Being away from Marc, away from her home—this was her parents' way of trying to prove they were right. *You can't handle it. You're not strong enough. You should come home.* Her appetite was gone.

*****

"Hey. How was your day?" Jennifer started the conversation.

She and Marc talked at least once each day, both trying valiantly to keep the lines of communication open. They knew that being able to talk was crucial to their marriage surviving.

"It was okay. Work sucked." Marc had been let go from his job at WLAF when they downsized, but was hired back roughly six months later. He no longer worried about his job security there but the atmosphere around the station was dismal. He told Jen about the latest staff meeting and jumped into his next thought prematurely, as was his nature.

"I was thinking about looking for a new job."

"Okay," Jen said. "Is someone hiring?"

"There's an opening in Charlottesville. What about there? Or I also saw a job in Havre de Grace." The first, in Virginia, offered a college town with a cosmopolitan feel. But located by the Chesapeake Bay, Havre de Grace would keep them in Maryland and offer a cheaper cost of living. Both appealed to Jen for different reasons.

"Go for it," she said. "Let's see what happens."

Marc started applying and Jen, for the first time in a long time, thought about a future with her husband that seemed brighter.

*****

"Where should we start today?" the therapist asked. Marc and Jennifer sat in her office, ready to delve into whatever discussion might help them move forward. They attended couple's therapy religiously, each committed to trying to make things work. Sometimes they seemed to be on relatively even ground, other times each felt disconnected and less than committed to their relationship. Therapy should have been a way to fix that.

The catch was that, while called "couple's therapy," the sessions were really more focused on Jen's mental health and Marc's involvement in helping her improve. So, they answered the questions that were asked but never really dove into the topics that they—as a couple—needed to discuss to heal their marriage. Still, they attended. Quitting would feel like they were giving up on each other.

Of course, the distance wasn't always present. Sometimes they'd each notice (separately) that they were having a good time, that things felt "normal," the way they felt before Marc announced his plan to transition. They'd catch glimpses of the "old" them, the couple they used to be, and it felt warm and welcoming and wonderful. And just as quickly, something would change and that comfort would disappear again, a fragile heirloom brought out of the cupboard and polished, only to be put back on a shelf and shut away.

Whether it was in bed or out to dinner, Jen sometimes felt like she was talking to a stranger. And then it would feel normal again, as though it always had.

It took Jen a very long time to figure out why. How could they be strangers? How could they sometimes feel like there was such a gulf, but so quickly feel so connected again? The answer jolted her one day like a sting of static electricity, sharp and out of nowhere.

*****

She was in the living room, the cat purring contentedly on the couch. A commercial came on, one with a stupid jingle that annoyed her each time she heard it. Jennifer flipped the channel and there was a life insurance commercial: the widow in black, crying into a handkerchief. It dawned on her like an epiphany; she was in mourning! She was grieving the loss of her spouse. How could that be? He was sitting in the next room, singing while he packed. He'd gotten the job in Charlottesville, Virginia, and would begin their move this weekend.

As she listened to his voice, Jen couldn't help feeling as though her spouse had died; she recognized the stages of grief that have been documented so thoroughly by anyone who's suffered a loss. She'd certainly experienced shock and denial, as well as pain, anger and depression.

She marveled at this realization. It would explain so much! As Marc brought his suitcase to the hall, she thought through it all. Why, only sometimes, would she feel he was such a complete stranger? And why was it that the rest of the time he was so familiar? She asked at their next therapy appointment.

"You've had a very gradual 'getting to know' each other process," her therapist explained. "Yes, Marc is a stranger of sorts, but you've awakened next to him morning after morning. At the same time, you've watched his physical changes morph one at a time. You've seen the facial hair come in, heard his voice get deeper. It's not like you woke up one morning and there he was."

It made a certain sort of sense, Jennifer thought. But what about the profound sense of loss she sometimes felt?

"While you've been welcoming Marc bit by bit, you've also been losing Marika," came the doctor's reply. "You're saying goodbye to her each day as you say hello to him. From the physical changes to the death of your dreams, you're navigating a loss right now. Everything you're feeling is normal."

A natural explanation. It seemed so simple, so sensible. And yet still so strange—especially when it came to defining her sense of self. Marc set his duffel bag next to the suitcase.

Ding. The sound from her cell phone interrupted Jen's reverie. She'd been folding laundry, putting his shirts next to the cat (who was fighting for space on the couch) and thinking about whether they might be able to afford to go out to celebrate Marc's new job. They were saving money toward trying for a baby, but it had been such a tough year. A nice romantic dinner would be a great way to mark the milestone. Jen put down the shirt she was folding and grabbed her phone to check her texts.

"Hey! Checking in on u. Heard M is going thru a sex change! Wow! Happy 4 him. But where does that leave u? u still the prettiest lesbian I know? :) Call me later!" Her friend Rebecca's text was flirty, like her, but troubling.

Where does *that leave me?* she thought. *He knows where he's going... who he is ... what does that make* me? It took her just a split-second before the answer hit her: *It makes me a loving and supportive wife. That's what it makes me.* She was furious. How dare her friends try to label her! Why did they feel like they needed to? She was Jen, same as she'd always been. Jennifer went back to folding the laundry, taking out her frustration on the socks as she paired them up.

*****

Eyes

Burning into my soul.
Staring, wondering, questioning
Who are you?
Peering through me when my back is turned;
Voyeurs of life.

It's dark behind these eyes,
Foggy and full of shadows.
I am afraid of the darkness
Playing tricks on me,
Blinding me.

I hate being watched.
Studied and examined from all angles.
You see something every time
Which view is right, which is true?

Magnify what you see,
And you'll find me.
Look closer and you
Will see what I see;
What I don't want to see.

Pools you can get lost in.
Sucked to the bottom,
Breath extinguished.
Stop staring; don't look at me!
You won't like what you find
You'll judge me
I know you will
It won't be pretty or kind.

I can't see!
I can't see you,
Until I see my way out of the dark.

*****

She brought it up at the next couple's therapy session. "Why do we have to have a label? What does that accomplish?" Jen asked, Marc nodding in agreement.

"People need to be able to categorize things," the doctor explained. "When we learn a language, we learn by putting labels on things. This is an apple. That is a school. People feel like they need to know how to categorize you."

"But what difference does it make?" Marc asked. "We may look like a heterosexual couple, but I don't feel like one. Do you?" he asked, turning to Jennifer.

"No, I don't," she said. "I'm not sure what I feel like. I just feel like us."

That felt so good. That realization: us. *We are* us, *just like we've always been*. She'd reached the sixth stage of grief: working through.

*****

"I'd like to talk with you about your identity," her therapist said at their next individual appointment. Jen sat in the familiar office, in the chair she always sat in—to the right of the doctor's desk. She faced the bookshelf with its many tomes, most of which had probably never been read.

"We spend a lot of time talking about Marc, and about how his transition impacts you. Today, I'd like to focus on how you feel about yourself."

Jen chuckled. "You mean outside of the scars on my body from cutting and trying to starve myself?" She didn't mean to be insolent; it was an emotional joke meant to cover her embarrassment.

"I mean ..." the doctor drew a breath. "How would you describe yourself today?"

A long pause ensued. How *did* she describe herself? A wife. A woman. A compassionate person. She figured that's not what the doctor was after.

"Well...I'm not sure what you mean."

"Would you still say you're a lesbian?" the doctor questioned.

Without hesitation, Jennifer nodded. "Yeah, I would. If it weren't for Marc, I'd be with a woman." She glanced around the room, looking for something else to focus on. This was not a pleasant conversation to be having. God, she hated to be classified like an object!

The doctor noticed her tension. "Have I upset you?"

Jen wasn't quite sure how to answer that. Was she upset? Or just uncomfortable? She paused a long while, gathering her thoughts. Her words came out even before she'd really processed them.

"I guess that, because I hadn't identified as a lesbian for very long before I met Mar...c (she still stumbled over his name sometimes), I didn't have much invested in being a lesbian. I mean, he kind of helped me discover myself. So yeah, I'm still a lesbian. I just happen to be in love with a man."

And that answered that, at least as far as Jennifer was concerned. Her friends could try to label her all they wanted. She knew who she was.

*****

Chapter 13
The Ties that Bind

"Can you bring in that last box from the car?" Jen was ready for the move to be over. Marc had already been in Charlottesville for a month, but Jen was just now joining him. Once he'd moved out, she'd stayed with her parents and kept working at the retinal specialists' office until she'd landed her own job in Virginia, working for a bankruptcy firm.

She was very much looking forward to their fresh start. New jobs, a new city—she felt more hopeful than she had in a very long time. This was a blank slate. No one knew them here. Marc was just Marc, not Marc-who-used-to-be-Marika. Their history was theirs alone. Here, they could be Marc and Jennifer Wyndham. No more, no less.

Of course, they'd met with some resistance when they discussed the move with Jen's parents. Cindy had expressed concern, reluctant to see her daughter move an entire state away. She was worried that Jen would be isolated and, alone, would sink back into the depression she'd so recently climbed out of. While the conversation hadn't been easy, Jennifer had assured her mom that this was what she wanted. A new beginning was just what she needed.

*****

Marc brought her the box tightly sealed with packing tape, neatly labeled in Jennifer's meticulous handwriting. Jen began emptying its contents: this one was mostly sheets and linens. As she put the towels in the bathroom closet, she spied Marc's chest binder hanging on the bathroom door. It was the bane of his existence.

Like a bra but a million times worse, a chest binder had been an essential part of Marc's wardrobe since his transition. He'd always hated his breasts, first hoping he wouldn't develop them at all, then hiding them for years under a loose-fitting shirt. They were yet another reminder of the body he was born with; the one that had never fit his mindset.

Meant to minimize the appearance of breasts, a binder fits snugly, like a corset, flattening the tissue to make the wearer appear as flat chested as possible. Tight, uncomfortable, and stifling, binders helped hide his breasts but were so uncomfortable. Marc couldn't wait to get home and take them off.

The trouble would arise when he had to put them back on.

"Marc, the pizza delivery guy is here. Can you grab that?"

"Hey honey, we're out of milk. Would you mind running out to get some?"

Whatever the reason was, it was never enough for him to want to put the damned thing back on. Besides the physical discomfort of it, it was a mental and emotional reminder that he'd been born in the wrong body. Marc hated his binder with a passion. Without it, he hid in the comfort of his own home. With it, he walked around feeling like someone was sitting on his chest all day. The instructions warned to wear them only four hours at a time; Marc wore his for eight hours a day at work, plus. It took its toll on him until he couldn't stand it anymore.

*****

He'd raised the issue from time to time over the years since he'd started his transition, and one night over dinner in their Charlottesville apartment, he brought it up again. They'd just gotten an order of Chinese food delivered, and Marc had just removed his binder.

"Babe, I know we've talked about this before, but what would you think if I were to get top surgery?" he asked. He'd thought about it so often, but had been fearful of bringing it up recently. They'd really just found some even ground after the move and Jen was so recently on the road to recovery following her mental illness. The last thing he wanted to do was rock the boat.

At the same time, the subject of children had also recently come up again. After so many years of waiting, Jen felt like she was ready to pursue having a baby. Marc too. He was completely on board with the idea, but the thought raised in him a new consideration—what would his child think of a father with boobs? He didn't want to hide his breasts in front of his child, but he also didn't want to have to explain things too soon. So, he asked the question that had been nagging at him.

Jen, as usual, took her time responding. She picked at her food, moving her shrimp around on her plate with her chopstick before answering. "Well, I'm not sure," she answered truthfully. She knew how much Marc hated the binder. It made it hard to breathe and often caused him back pain. She also knew how his breasts reminded him of the body he'd been born with. But she was very well aware of the potential risks—and costs—of surgery, and she wasn't looking forward to facing either of them.

Top surgery, also called gender reassignment, results in a more masculine chest. It involves breast removal and chest contouring, along with nipple grafts. They had discussed the topic several times before, but always in a nebulous, "one-day" kind of mentality. Now, it appeared "one-day" was here, and Jen wasn't sure she was ready. Not because she didn't want him to. It had nothing to do with that. She was fully supportive of him doing what he needed to do to be happy—that much should have already been apparent.

But Jennifer knew that the surgery was expensive, and they'd been trying to save money once his transition was complete. She'd believed their growing savings account meant they were ready to start a family, not pay for cosmetic surgery.

She finally put her words together carefully. "I want you to be happy. You know that."

Marc sensed the "but" before Jennifer said it. "But…" he prodded.

"But I thought we were saving for our baby!"

"I know, I *know*," he responded. And he *did* know. He wanted a child too. It wasn't that he'd changed his mind or anything. He just couldn't see how he could feel like a real father when he had to hide *breasts*, for God's sake.

"Let me think about it," Jen said. The subject was closed. For now.

*****

Lying in bed, Jennifer let the disappointment wash over her freely, without filtering it. She was disappointed. How could this happen *again*? How was it fair that she had to keep putting *her* life on hold for Marc's dreams? She felt like, once again, what she wanted would be glossed over so that Marc could be happy. And to give him that happiness, it meant she once again had to put what she wanted on the back burner.

*****

"It's not fair!" she told her therapist as soon as she sat down. Jen knew she sounded a bit like a four-year-old, but she had to share her frustration with someone. Her new therapist in Charlottesville was the person most likely to understand.

"I get it," the therapist responded. "This must be a real blow to you."

It was, on so many levels: some of them not even apparent to Jennifer yet. She understood Marc's discomfort. She related to him wanting to have the surgery before a child. And yet, once again, it felt like it didn't matter what Jennifer wanted or needed. She felt resentment creep back into her thoughts.

"What does this mean to you? Personally, I mean," her therapist said.

The answer could go a thousand different ways. It meant she wasn't as important. It meant he always came first. It meant putting off their family— yet again. And, to her surprise, it meant something she hadn't yet identified.

"Why is it that *Marc* can do whatever he wants to his body, and everyone is okay with that? But when I treat my body the way I want to, everyone freaks out? How is that fair?" Copious tears streamed down her face.

The therapist handed her the box of tissues. "It's not," she said kindly. "But it is different."

Jennifer failed to see how.

*****

The move to Charlottesville had been good for a number of reasons. For the first time, Jennifer was seeing a dietician, Cheryl, who specialized in eating disorders. Cheryl had battled—and beaten—her own eating disorder, making her an ally who completely understood the war from every angle. Jen took an instant liking to her.

The relocation also resulted in an unexpected shift in Jennifer's relationship with her mother. Now that the pair was separated by a four-hour drive, it required both Cindy and Jen to make more of an effort to see each other. Unless Cindy had fully embraced Marc's transition, it would have been easy for her to drift out of Jen's life. Jen was thankful to see a definite effort on her mom's part to wholly accept Marc as a man. From using the correct pronouns to calling him "Marc," Cindy had come around. Jen felt their relocation had been the catalyst that had gotten their relationship back on track.

*****

Jen and Marc took advantage of their new surroundings to immerse themselves in community theatre. Jen had performed in several shows before they moved, Marc just a few. Both were eager to get back onstage.

The couple was cast in a local production of a musical called "The Producers," and both looked forward to working together and strengthening their relationship via a common interest. Rehearsals were fun; the cast was receptive and both Jennifer and Marc enjoyed their new theatre family. But Jen soon found herself facing some familiar feelings.

"You'll be wearing a dress that's tight fitting, but will allow you to dance," the costumer said, as she measured Jen's waist. Almost instantly, Jennifer felt her pulse quicken. She resolved to make sure the costume would look okay on her.

*****

Jen fought to keep her caloric intake under control. The stress and anxiety of how she'd look onstage dictated her diet, and she returned to her old standbys: eating less and purging when necessary to take control of the scale.

Marc noticed her behavior but didn't say much about it. He was in a no-win situation. If he policed her, she got resentful. If he said nothing, she would starve herself.

This time, though, Jen had a secret weapon: her dietician. Cheryl acted as a buffer and, when necessary, a bully. She took the burden off of

Marc, who no longer felt he had to monitor his wife's eating. And, almost miraculously, she made Jen feel accountable for her actions; if Cheryl was going to put in the work to help Jen get better, Jen felt she had to at least try to meet Cheryl halfway. While Jen lost weight during the show, she kept it within acceptable limits.

*****

Jennifer met up with Vivian, a new friend from work, for a coffee one afternoon. It was June, and the Virginia heat was just starting to climb to the uncomfortable levels. This particular day was breezy and nice, though, and they sat outside enjoying the lazy warmth of late-day sun.

Jennifer sipped her coffee as Vivian prattled away. She was somewhat distracted, still mulling over her latest conversation with Marc. He'd brought up the top surgery again. She wasn't ready to hear it yet, and she'd told him so.

".... and then Janice said ... Jennifer, are you listening?" Vivian asked.

"Yep, sorry!" she laughed, trying to hide her lack of interest. How on earth was she supposed to care about the latest news among their office mates when she was faced with her situation. She tried to pay better attention as Vivian continued.

In no time at all, though, her attention drifted again. She saw a woman outside pushing a stroller, only the baby's head visible. A sweet pink and blue striped cap was identifiable—this was a newborn, fresh from the hospital, fresh from the womb. Jennifer's heart clutched.

I *want* that! *I. Want. That!* She screamed silently.

And as she watched, a man came up to the woman, carefully handing her a coffee cup with a brown cardboard sleeve so she wouldn't burn her fingers on the hot container. The woman gently took it from him with both hands as he leaned over the stroller and grinned at his newborn. He looked every bit the proud papa: strong, confident, and comfortable.

And with that, Jennifer *knew*.

She knew Marc needed the surgery, and now she understood he needed it before he became a father. Marc was making changes to his body to make him mentally healthy, to enable him to the best father he could be. The changes she'd made to her body were anything but healthy—mentally or physically.

Finally, she understood. Marc should have the surgery.

*****

Paying for it was a different matter. They estimated that the surgery and related expenses would be around $6,000. Their credit was horrible. They'd both been unemployed for a time right around Jen's hospitalizations, and they'd racked up a staggering amount of credit card debt. They certainly didn't have enough in savings to cover the entire cost. They knew they'd need someone to co-sign a loan. Marc asked his stepdad first.

"I'm happy to help you with it, as soon as we buy the new house," his stepdad said.

Marc's mom and stepfather had found a house they loved in Florida and needed to get through closing before they'd be able to assist. They estimated it would take a few months before they'd be in a position to co-sign the loan.

Jennifer watched Marc's mood closely and knew waiting was not an option. She knew the signs of depression, and she worried that her husband was slowly entering that black hole. He *felt* like a man. He sounded masculine. His facial hair certainly made him look like a male. But his breasts were an everyday reminder to him that his outer appearance didn't match his mindset.

Jennifer came up with an idea. "Why don't you ask Tom?" she suggested. Tom and Marc had been friends for so long and gone through so much together; it was a perfectly logical suggestion. Marc resisted at first, unable or unwilling to ask his friend to help him out. But as his depression worsened, he knew he needed to set his pride aside and ask for assistance.

Marc needn't have worried.

"Absolutely," Tom said, almost before Marc even finished asking the question. "I'm happy to co-sign for you."

With Tom's signature added to theirs, Marc and Jen applied for a loan that would change their lives. They waited for the good news that their request had been accepted.

Except it wasn't. The bank denied their request—their debt-to-income ratio was too high. It was a blow, but not for long.

"Hey bud," Marc said. He'd called Tom to tell him the bad news.

"What's happening? Ready to go have surgery?" Tom asked.

"Not exactly."

Marc shared the bank's decision.

Without hesitation, Tom spoke. "So, I'll just loan you the money."

"What?" Marc was stunned. Jennifer, from across the room, looked on, trying to determine what was happening based on Marc's reaction.

"I've got it. I'll just loan it to you. You can pay me back but that way you don't have to wait."

They couldn't believe it! Just like that, hope returned. Marc was ecstatic. He called his stepdad to tell him about Tom's grand gesture.

But by now, his stepdad had a surprise of his own. "We're nearly done with the house stuff. I'll give Tom half of the money so he's not out of pocket for all of it. You can just pay both of us as you can."

Just like that, they'd come up with a way to finance it all. Marc's top surgery was a go.

*****

"Hello, doctor's office," the receptionist answered.

"Hi, um, I need to make a payment on an account."

"What's your name?" the receptionist asked.

"Well, my name is Tom, but the patient's name is Marc Wyndham."

The nurse paused. "Are you a relative?" She wasn't quite sure how to handle this one.

"No, just a friend," Tom responded.

"And you want to make a payment on Mr. Wyndham's account?"

"Yep. In fact, I want to pay it off."

"You're gonna pay for the *whole thing*?"

"Yeah, I am. He's my best friend, and he needs this surgery and doesn't have the money for it so I told him I'd pay for it."

"Well aren't you something?" the receptionist said. "Imagine that. I could use some friends like you!" she laughed and took down Tom's financial information.

And with the processing of a credit card, the surgery was paid for.

*****

Marc's surgeon was in Florida, which meant he and Jen could stay with his mom and stepdad to cut down on expenses before and after the surgery. They wouldn't have to foot a hotel bill on top of everything else. They packed their bags and headed to the airport.

Jennifer worried about the surgery simply because of the general risks.

Anesthesia. Infection. Any number of things could go wrong. She worried about all of them.

Marc, on the other hand, couldn't have been more excited about it. They sat in the terminal at the airport, waiting to be called to board the flight to Tampa. They people watched, mostly, commenting on passersby and trying to guess where they were flying and why.

"She's meeting her lover here so they can fly to Cancun for a little sumpin' sumpin'," Marc surmised, about a pretty lady with a straw hat and an oversized pink suitcase.

Jen tried to one-up him. "And *he's* the lover." She pointed to a wizened old man sitting across the terminal from them. It helped to pass the time and to calm Jennifer's nerves. Soon enough, their flight was announced, and they walked toward the plane, ready to take the next step on their journey together.

*****

The pre-op appointment was brief and uneventful. Forms, forms, and more forms for Marc to complete. Jennifer just chuckled—she knew the feeling all too well, line after line to fill out, and it seemed like every form asked the same questions as the last.

As he started in on yet another one, the bell jingled on the door. A man entered, arriving to check in for his appointment. Marc overheard him tell the receptionist he was there for a post-op visit. He was trans! Marc watched as the man chatted with her, the joy on his face evident.

And a minute later, the nurse called out for another patient. As the man next to Marc stood and headed to greet her, the nurse asked, "How's everything been going since the operation? Any problems?" Marc didn't hear the answer, but the question confirmed the guy had been another trans patient who'd had top surgery. The encounters with these others, so clearly overjoyed with their results, only ratcheted up Marc's excitement even more.

At last it was their turn. The nurse had barely spoken his last name before Marc was up and out of his chair, anxious to get started. He'd had blood work done back in Virginia to streamline the process, so this was their chance to meet the surgeon, ask questions, and give the doctor a chance to examine Marc before his surgery.

Like so many doctors' offices they'd been in together, it was a fairly unremarkable space, but as Marc climbed on the exam table he couldn't help but see it with fresh eyes. While he'd undergone the hormone aspect of his transition, he truly saw this top surgery as the beginning of a new life. His body would finally match the gender in his mind.

The doctor completed his exam. Prior to today, he'd only seen pictures of Marc's breasts—this was his first chance to see firsthand what he'd be operating on.

"It's a pretty straight-forward procedure," he explained. The doctor said he'd be performing something called a double-incision surgery, in which he'd make two horizontal incisions on Marc's chest, at the top and the bottom of the pectoral muscle. He explained that he'd pull the skin back, remove the breast tissue, and perform additional liposuction to adjust the contour.

Marc asked about nipple grafting, which he also wanted to have done, and the doctor walked him through that process, as well. He'd remove Marc's nipples, re-size them, and graft them back on once the rest of the surgery had been completed. He warned that Marc might feel limited sensation in his nipples following the surgery—an effect that was common with this approach.

The surgery was scheduled for the next day, and would last 3–4 hours. Marc would undergo general anesthesia for the procedure.

"You'll have medical drains that will be located under each arm," the doctor explained. "They're there to drain excess lymphatic fluid and blood. You'll have those for a week or so, and you'll have to empty them a few times a day. Are you up for that?"

Jen and Marc nodded.

"Healing will take a few weeks, and you won't be able to do any heavy lifting during that time. You'll have bandages to protect the area, and we'll remove those at your one-week post-op visit."

"What about scarring?" Jen asked the physician. Her one concern was that, after all of this, Marc still wouldn't be comfortable taking his shirt off in public, whether it be at the beach or in a theatre dressing room.

"The scars will be pretty noticeable for the first six weeks, but they will gradually fade and flatten over time," he said. "After 12-18 months, you'll have a very good idea of how they will look for the rest of your life. Any other questions?"

Marc and Jen were satisfied. The doctor was an expert in this area and had been very thorough. They felt like they knew all they needed to about how it would be handled and what to expect. Besides, Marc was impatient to get started.

"Can we just go do it right now?" he joked, and they all laughed. His enthusiasm was contagious, and Jennifer loved how excited her husband was. It was a good reminder they were doing the right thing with this surgery.

The nurse provided them with last-minute directions on what he could eat and when. Each listened carefully, following every word. They left the office with more instructions and a surgery time: 10:00 am the following day.

It was an outpatient procedure, which meant Jen, his mom and stepdad would be able to wait during the surgery. Marc's folks paid for a nearby hotel room for them to stay in that first night following surgery, so they wouldn't have to make a road trip back to Tampa right away.

The nurse advised them to arrive an hour and a half early so they could prep Marc. It was nearly time to take the final step in Marc's transition.

*****

Jen, Marc's mom and his stepfather sat in the waiting room, killing time. As they waited anxiously for news from the doctor, Jen thought back over all they'd come through to this point. From his name change and hormone therapy to her self-injury and anorexia, they'd each taken turns being both caretaker and patient. While they'd each struggled with their own demons along the way, they'd both had times of strength and struggle. The key was, neither of them had never given up on the other. She couldn't imagine going through this experience with anyone but Marc.

*****

Jen checked her texts to find one from Olivia, a woman she wasn't very close to. A lesbian, Olivia was very proud of her sexuality. They weren't particularly good friends, but they'd stayed loosely connected over the years. Jen didn't know how Olivia had heard about Marc's surgery but news travels, and it had made its way to Olivia's ear.

"So, M's getting them cut off? I hear that's really painful! I hope he's not expecting you to empty the drains. Yuck," Olivia texted.

It was another chance for others to question a decision that Jennifer herself hadn't made. *None of your damn business!* Jen thought, as she deleted the text without responding. First, she couldn't figure out why people thought it was her place to explain. And second, why were people so interested in her private life? That continued to baffle her.

*****

Surgery took longer than expected. Jen walked next door to eat at the hospital cafeteria, trying to read a book while she waited. Her thoughts kept drifting, though, as she imagined how happy Marc would be once it was over. She wondered whether she'd be able to touch his chest without him pulling away. To calm her nerves, she focused on that hope: the chance for a renewed sense of intimacy because he would no longer be reminded of body parts that didn't belong there.

She returned to the waiting room hopeful, eager, and nervous.

At long last, the doctor came out to see them. All had gone as planned. Marc's top surgery had been a success.

*****

Marc was loopy on the way back to his folk's house in Tampa the day after surgery. The pain drugs were working their magic, and as he watched the scenery flash by from the passenger seat, he dozed off and on. The nurses had shown Jen what she needed to do to empty the drains (take *that*, Olivia!), and she did it dutifully every day for the first week before flying home. She needed to head back to work, but Marc was staying to recover for an extra week thanks to his mom and stepdad's help.

The most annoying part to Marc was the Ace bandage that was tightly wound around his chest. He'd spent years forcing himself into binders, flattening, adjusting and hiding his breasts. He'd been ready to be done with it—only to have this damn bandage squeezing him day in and day out following surgery. He knew he only had to wear it for a week, but each of those seven days felt like a lifetime.

His post-op visit was on Halloween, and as Marc walked into the doctor's office for his check-up, he found it hysterically ironic—he actually felt like a mummy. The nurse escorted him into the room, flicking the lights on as she went. She closed the door and got to work removing his bandages and the drains. Marc's anticipation built by the moment. It would be his first chance to see the surgical results. At last, the unveiling was complete, and the nurse turned Marc toward the corner of the room where a full-length mirror was positioned.

"I'll give you a moment alone and come back shortly," she said, and closed the door behind her.

Marc just stared at himself in the mirror. He couldn't believe what he saw—and what he didn't. The scars were extremely noticeable, of course: thin lines on both sides of his chest. A square bandage covered each of his nipples. But he saw past them to the potential of what he'd look like when he healed. It was surreal, and honestly felt like a dream. He took a quick picture of himself with his phone and went back to staring.

How can removing a part of me make me feel whole? he wondered, but that was exactly how he felt. Alone in the empty exam room, Marc finally felt complete. Validated. And for the first time in his life, thoroughly male.

*****

Jen called to check in after his one-week post-op visit. "How'd it go?" she asked, juggling the phone in one hand and the bag of groceries in the other.

"Awesome!" he said. "I mean, they still feel pretty sore because of the surgery, but they look so good! Wait 'til you see me!" The happiness in his voice was palpable—and infectious.

Jennifer found herself responding in kind. "I'm so glad! I wish I could've been there with you."

"It's all good," Marc said. "Miss you!"

"Miss you too, babe," Jen said, and meant it.

Marc flew home a week later, and Jen saw the surgical scars for the first time without the bandage to buffer them. They looked raw and painful. The old fear crept back into her thoughts: *what if he's unhappy with the scarring? What if he's still not comfortable taking his top off at the pool or in front of our kid?* But Marc seemed happier than she'd seen him in a very long time, and gradually, she let herself accept that he was going to heal fine, and, equally important, that surgery was absolutely the right move.

*****

Marc pushed the cat out of the way and scooted closer to Jennifer. This was the second time this week he'd made an overture toward sex, and she sighed both with pleasure and relief. She knew it was hard for her friends to understand, but in some ways, she found herself more attracted to him now than ever. Their bond and their shared struggles had made them closer, and she relished the fact that they could express themselves with each other again. *Intimacy comes from within, I guess,* Jen thought as she turned off the light and reached out to make love to her husband.

*****

Chapter 14
Looking Ahead at What's Behind

"How can I help you?" The fertility doctor was tall, thin, and up in years. Probably in his 70s; he reminded them of the stereotypical doctor you'd see on an episode of Marcus Welby. With kind eyes behind his wire-rimmed glasses, he was calm and calming. And he was their best hope at having a baby.

Jennifer got right to the point. "My husband is transgender, so we need to use donor insemination, and as far as I know, I'm healthy," she blurted out. But she was excited, nervous, and ready to move forward with their dream that had been put on hold for so long. She found herself scared of the doctor's response. After all, he was of a very different generation, and it was entirely feasible he wouldn't be supportive of their marriage.

"Okay," the doctor responded. "We can work with that."

Relief flooded through Jen's veins. This office, this very normal, unassuming doctor's office, would be where their journey to have a baby began. *It's about time*, Jen thought.

******

They had talked about having a baby before they'd gotten engaged. Marika had brought up the idea first. As usual, timing was not her strong suit. Impulsive as a ten-year-old, she really wanted to know where Jennifer stood on the matter. "So, what do you think about kids?" she threw the idea out there one night during dinner. They'd only been dating for a few months, but Marika already knew she wanted to raise kids. She also knew *she* didn't want to be the one to carry a baby.

Jen took a sip of water before responding. Yes, she'd thought about being a mother. Yes, she really felt deeply about Marika. But she wasn't sure she was ready for this conversation just yet. "Well," she drew out the word a bit, buying herself time. "I do think I want children but I definitely want to be married first."

Unwilling to let the conversation go, Marika pushed. "But, like, would you wanna carry the baby?" She waited impatiently for an answer, fiddling with her sleeve while Jen considered her response.

"Yeah, probably. I guess." It seemed a bit soon to be discussing this, but she wanted to give Marika an answer.

Despite the lack of enthusiasm, that was enough for Marika. She wouldn't have to have a baby coming out of her vagina. *Cool*, she thought. *That's settled.*

******

Of course, that was just the first conversation. Once they got engaged, Jennifer was totally on board with the idea of having a baby—and with being the one who carried it. She could see them as a great little family: she and Marika walking through the mall, two moms showing off their beautiful bundle of joy and dirty diapers—*If I'm going through pregnancy and delivery, Marika gets that part*, she thought. She envisioned all of the traditional milestones of parenthood: kissing boo boos and celebrating birthdays and putting cookies out for Santa. Jen was not only on board with having a baby, she was excited about it and ready to make it happen.

Marc's decision to transition had put all of that on hold for six very long years. They'd waited through the transition, waited until after Marc's top surgery was complete, and waited until they had enough money saved to start the process. The conversation had come up time and again, but they hadn't ever been at a point where they could start the process. With their marriage (and their bank account) on track, it was finally time.

******

They went straight from the doctor's office down the hall for Jennifer to get an ultrasound. The test was routine—a way for the doctor to be sure that there were no obvious obstacles to Jen being able to conceive. Standard blood work was the next step, and then the couple headed home to make a choice that would impact the rest of their lives: it was time to select a sperm donor.

Because Marc's mother was Japanese (his father was Caucasian), they decided from the start to look for a donor who was half Japanese. Their hope was that would give the baby the best chance of representing both of them. Jennifer was willing let Marc take the lead on the donor selection, since she would carry the child. When he would find a potential donor, the two of them would pore over the information, imagining their child fathered by that candidate.

"Ooh, what about this one?" Marc would say, finding a suitable donor bio. Or, "This one's write-up reads like he could be a serial killer. Maybe we ought to skip him." Sharing the selection process was a heady time, filled with anticipation and hope. Choosing a donor brought them even closer, underscoring the fact that they were focused on a future *together*.

Their list of qualifications wasn't too stringent other than the half-Japanese requirement; the only other real quality they sought was someone who had a creative side—perhaps involved in music or art, dance or theatre—so that the baby would have a chance of inheriting those interests that were also so important to Marc and Jen. Whittling down the available donors was akin to choosing a new car: which one best fit the criteria but also just *felt* right.

Jennifer wasn't worried about the ultrasound or the blood test she'd undergone. She had no reason to expect that anything was other than normal. Which is why, when the phone rang, she answered brightly and without hesitation.

"Is this Mrs. Wyndham?" the voice questioned.

"Yes, this is she."

"Hi, it's Dr. Adams." Jennifer mouthed the word *"doctor"* to Marc across the room.

"I wanted to discuss your test results with you. Your ultrasound came back fine. We see no obvious reasons you'd have difficulty carrying a baby to term."

"Oh good," Jen answered, giving Marc a thumbs-up sign.

"But we do need to discuss your blood work. Are you familiar with a virus called CMV?"

Jen shook her head, too late realizing the doctor couldn't see her. "No," she whispered, her heart firmly in her throat. Marc heard the change in her voice and looked up, growing concerned.

"It's a common virus. Most people have had it without even realizing it and have already built up antibodies to it naturally. Your blood work shows you've never had it, though."

"Oh, that's good then, right?"

"What it means is that you'll need to find a donor that is also CMV negative. Otherwise, you run the risk of contracting the virus while you're pregnant and then passing it on to your baby, which could be dangerous."

Jen absorbed the news, trying to make sure she understood what the doctor was saying. "So, it's not a bad thing?" she questioned.

"No, absolutely not," came the doctor's reply. "It simply needs to be part of the criteria when you are selecting a sperm donor."

"Okay, got it. Thank you, doctor," Jen said.

"Let me know when you've found a candidate." With that, the doctor hung up, and Jen turned to Marc with new criteria to add to their search.

As it turned out, the news made their search pretty simple. There were already a limited number of half-Japanese donors available and now that they also needed to find one who was CMV negative, it narrowed it down to two candidates at the cryo bank in California where they had begun their search. For twenty-five dollars, they purchased a full profile of one of the donors, which came with his baby picture, so they could imagine a child with those features crossed with Jennifer's. Liking everything they saw, they made their choice: Donor number one.

******

As Marc and Jennifer would soon learn, everything about baby making came down to timing. (Ironically, everything about their life together, so far, mirrored that very same element.) From accurately predicting ovulation by taking a prediction test to having the insemination appointment scheduled within a short window—it all relied on the timing being exactly perfect.

When her ovulation prediction test indicated the time was right, Jen called the doctor's office and made her appointment for later that same day. Marc picked her up and they headed to the lab to sign out their sample. (They were also soon to learn just how careful doctors' offices are when it comes to protecting sperm samples.) After confirming their identities about a half-dozen times, they were finally given the small vial that held their future in the form of a swimming spermatozoa.

"Now, you be sure and keep that warm," the nurse advised as she handed it over. "It needs to stay at body temperature to keep the sperm viable."

Jen held it tightly in her hand, shaking both with adrenaline and nerves. The vial had already been thawing for ten minutes, and it was crucial to handle it properly. The nurse told them where the waiting room was, and together they made their way down the brightly lit hall. Paintings lined the walls along the way: flowers, mountains, sunrise over a farm. The images were probably meant to be soothing, but they did nothing to tame Jennifer's excitement.

Marc, equally animated, tried to calm her as they waited. "Relax," he repeated numerous times. "You need to calm down." And a second later, he'd ask, "Are you keeping it warm?" She smiled at him—he was no calmer than she, even if he tried to pretend otherwise.

A nurse came and ushered them into a room with a table and a bright light overhead. Jen climbed onto the table in her hospital gown, too anxious to sit still. The doctor arrived a few minutes later and described to them exactly what to expect. He'd insert a thin tube into Jennifer's uterus and inject a saline rinse to clear the tube, and then they'd inject the semen and hope it did its job. That was it. Jen held still as the procedure was carried out, staring at the wall where a framed People magazine cover featured Ellen DeGeneres.

"And now, you'll need to lie flat and wait twenty minutes to help give the swimmers time to do their thing," the nurse explained, once the doctor had left. "I'll be back to let you know when the time is up."

Alone in the room, Marc and Jennifer burst out laughing. Nothing was funny, but their pent-up energy needed somewhere to go. They killed time watching YouTube and joking. The time passed pretty quickly, both of them wired and giddy from adrenaline at this new step they were taking. It was real—they were making their dream come true.

******

The next two weeks passed about as slowly as any two weeks ever had. Jen crossed off the days on the calendar in the kitchen, an X to mark the passage of time until she could take a pregnancy test and find out if they'd been successful. Not many people knew they'd begun treatments, but those who did checked in often to see if there was any news. Marc and Jen went to work as though each day were normal instead of part of a countdown to the biggest test of their lives.

At last, the two-week mark arrived. Jen woke first and made her way to her bathroom. Their small apartment had two—they'd agreed from the get-go they'd each have their own, enabling Jen to enjoy keeping hers tidy while Marc's reflected his more casual style. She sat down on the toilet, pregnancy test in hand, said a quick prayer, and waited for the result.

Marc could tell from the way she opened the door that it hadn't been positive. "It's okay, babe. We knew the first time would be a long shot. They told us it usually takes three to four times."

Jennifer sighed. She knew that. He was right, of course. But a small part of her still hoped the test was wrong. Maybe she'd taken it too soon? Maybe she should take another test in a couple of days. Sadly, her period arrived right on schedule, confirming the test's accuracy. They'd have to try again.

******

Money was tight at that point, and the couple had covered the costs of the first insemination attempt with their tax return. It was not an inexpensive proposition. Between the sperm sample itself, the specialized temperature controlled shipping, and delivery fees, Marc and Jen had spent about $1,000 on their first, failed attempt to get pregnant. They'd have to save up before they could try a second time. By cutting household costs and living frugally, they were able to foot the bill again in May, just two months later.

It all felt exactly the same: the multiple confirmation of their identities ("Your name and date of birth, please."); the walk down the hallway with its myriad paintings; the People magazine with Ellen on the cover; the same procedure, twenty minutes lying flat on the table. And two weeks later, the same result. The only thing that changed was the reaction—which was an amped up, more intense disappointment when the pregnancy test showed the outcome of their efforts. Well-meaning friends—the few who knew—and their parents offered consolation and encouragement. They all had good intentions, but unfortunately, they couldn't make it better. And with the expense of the procedure, Marc and Jen agreed they needed to wait awhile before trying again. They'd stretched themselves too thin by trying again so soon. They'd have to put off a third attempt for several months. Once again, a baby would have to wait.

******

The summer passed mostly uneventfully, with one significant exception: for the first time, Marc was able to go to swimming, shirtless, at the neighborhood pool.

It was your ordinary community pool, with shallow and deep ends with a separate baby pool off to the side. They'd been there before, of course. Both enjoyed swimming and warming themselves in the sun. But Marc had always had his binder on before, which meant he stayed covered up. All the other men thought nothing of taking off their shirts and jumping in. He'd always envied them, imagining the feeling of freedom that must provide, and longing to feel the warm sun on his naked shoulders. Since he'd had his top surgery there was no reason he couldn't do the same.

It was heaven! Such a simple thing, but to Marc, it represented more than just swimming without a shirt. It was liberating to feel the water brush his skin, to lie back on the lounge chair with the sun drying him. He was a bit self-conscious about the surgical scars the very first time, but the freeing feeling quickly helped him overcome that. Jen watched him, at first amused and then solidly happy for him. His confidence—and comfort—was evident. He was truly at peace with his body for the first time in his life, and she couldn't have been more thrilled for him. Her own troubles with his decision to transition seemed so very long ago, and as she jumped in the water and splashed him, it was so obvious that they were meant to be together: a loving couple, man and wife.

******

Summer drew to a close, the long days shortening and the hot, humid Virginia August giving way to a slightly cooler and only slightly less humid September. While they hadn't been talking much about a baby for several months it was never far from top of mind for either of them. Come October, their bank account and their mental fortitude seemed ready for another attempt. Jen called the doctor.

"I remember you saying something about a drug I could take that might help us conceive," she said.

"Yes, that would be Clomid, which is frequently prescribed after a third unsuccessful attempt. It's safe and has proven to be fairly successful for many patients."

In a move that was very un-Jen-like, she persisted. "I know we've only tried twice but I'm thirty-four, and we don't have a lot of extra money to keep trying. Could you prescribe the Clomid for me before we try this again?"

The doctor agreed, and also suggested a new type of ultrasound with dye that would show whether Jennifer's fallopian tubes were open—a common cause for women who have difficulty getting pregnant. Jen agreed. As it turned out, her reproductive organs were right as rain. The previous attempts just hadn't worked for whatever reason.

But she had extra ammunition—Clomid—and she was banking on the third time being the charm.

******

The third time was anything but charming. The Clomid had a wicked effect on Jennifer. She took it for seven days, each one of them worse than the last. Jen, who'd come so far in terms of her mental health, was a weepy, sobbing mess. Hopeless and hurting, she retreated into a shell of depression in a matter of days. Marc watched, horrified, as his wife morphed into a basket case right in front of his eyes.

And as he watched her deteriorate mentally, there was more work to be done. As it turns out, donor number one was no longer an option—he'd stopped donating his sperm, and there was none left to ship to them. They'd have to choose another donor. The California-based cryobank didn't have anyone that matched their qualifications, so Marc and Jennifer explored a sperm bank much closer to home in Virginia. While there weren't any half-Japanese donors, they found a half-Korean donor who, like Jen, was CMV-negative. He also liked cooking and music, both of which appealed to the couple. They sent away for his full profile and baby picture, and liked what they saw. Marc and Jen had found their choice. Donor number two was chosen.

Both of them went into their third attempt with equal amounts of hope and caution. Jen, more than Marc, fully expected this time to be successful. She willed it to work as she was lying on the table and looking at the poster of Ellen. *You will work. I will be pregnant. We will get a baby this time.*

She was wrong.

******

Of course, they tried again. It took every bit of savings, but they decided to do it the next month: November. A time to be thankful. Jen, tired of being disappointed, resisted getting her hopes up. But Marc remained optimistic. Surely, this would be their chance to have a baby.

One thing was for certain: Jennifer would never take Clomid again. While it was only for seven days, the effect had been so dramatic that Marc insisted Jen ask the doctor for an alternative. Seeing his wife in that state had scared him badly. He couldn't bear to see her go through that again.

This time, the doctor prescribed Femara, which caused very few side effects for Jennifer. She took the full seven-day dose and resolutely made the appointment to go in to the doctor's office when her ovulation test came back positive. "Whatever," she thought, as she waited out the twenty minutes on the table after the procedure. The giddiness was gone. This was self-preservation—she wouldn't allow herself to be disappointed again.

******

Jen held the pregnancy stick in her hand, making sure that her aim was good, and finished up. There was no need to prolong her bathroom visit and certainly no need to freak out over it. She'd been through that too many times. She flushed, heading back to bed to wait for the results. She thought about their plans for the day: grocery shopping, picking up the ingredients for the pie she was supposed to bring to her mom's for Thanksgiving, cleaning the apartment. Her mind filled the space where her hope should have been, detailing the minutia of day-to-day life. And just as she expected, when she made her way back to the bathroom, there was no plus sign on the damned stick.

"Nope," she called out to Marc, still in bed. She brushed her teeth and turned to flip the light off.

Something made her look again. "Wait a minute...."

Marc had never moved so fast.

"I think... maybe... It's hard to say, but I *think* that's a plus sign."

It was really hard to tell. The pink against the white was so faint that it was possible they were just imagining what they wanted to see. Marc had an idea.

"Hang on," he said. "Lemme get my camera." Rushing through the apartment, he grabbed his phone and took a picture of the test, this innocuous stick that held so much promise. He used his camera to invert the colors to black and white. Sure enough, a faint plus sign showed up.

******

After all they'd been through, it was hard to believe it. Positive. She was pregnant! Seeking more validation, they piled into the car and drove to the all-night drug store to buy another test. It was only 6:30 am, and Jennifer was still in her pajamas, but Marc ran into the store and bought three different kinds of tests. *If one is good, surely three are better, right?* They drove home—ecstatic, unbelieving, hopeful.

They decided to try the more advanced test, a digital one this time. Instead of having to try to see if there was a plus sign or not, this would tell them definitively: "pregnant" or "not." It was an excruciating two minutes. Neither of them spoke as both contemplated what this could mean. Finally, it was time. Marc went in to check. From the bathroom, his voice echoed back to her across the apartment.

"I don't want you to be upset... this test specifically said it was meant to be taken later on. So, it's probably just too early."

Jen felt her hopes deflate. It had been too good to be true. She knew it.

"But it says 'Pregnant!'" he called out.

Jen screamed, and Marc ran out to wrap her in a hug. It was true. They were going to be parents! As Marc sank to the floor on his knees, Jen thought about how far they'd come—alone and together. They were going to be parents. They were finally going to have their baby.

No more looking back. It was time to plan the future.

Chapter 15
And Baby Makes Three

Brushing her teeth was the worst. The mint-flavored toothpaste made Jennifer gag terribly, until she was nearly ready to give up good dental hygiene for the next nine months. A few cavities would be worth it if she didn't feel like vomiting each time she brushed. But full-on morning sickness soon followed, and she could no longer blame it on the paste. Now, many things had to be avoided; even decaf coffee and water upset her stomach. Chocolate almond milk became her new BFF in the morning—it was the only thing she could reliably keep down.

Jen recognized that between the morning sickness and the fatigue, she was going to need to let her boss in on the secret. Jen shared the news with him fairly early on in the pregnancy. She knew it was risky to tell anyone this soon but she thought if she was feeling so poorly already, it could get worse before it got better, and she hoped to lessen the stress of missing work.

Fortunately, he was pleased for her and very supportive. "Do what you need to do to take care of yourself," he advised. "If that means you come in later, or miss a day and make it up on the weekends, I'm fine with that."

It was a relief and a welcomed bit of advice. She was often tired due to anemia that couldn't seem to be controlled despite the iron supplements she took.

The pregnancy progressed pretty normally. She and Marc delighted in sharing the news with friends and family. They planned the nursery, packed a hospital bag, and prepared themselves as best they could for the changes that were about to happen. They decided they wanted to find out the gender before the birth. Actually, they thought they already knew, based on both their own instincts and how many times people had predicted it: they were having a girl. The old wives' tales all seemed to be in agreement, and when they went to Jen's twenty-two-week ultrasound they were fully prepared to hear it officially.

After confirming they wanted to know the gender, the ultrasound tech announced cheerfully, "It's a boy!"

"A boy?" All thoughts of anticipating a girl immediately left Jennifer's mind. Of *course* they were having a boy. It just seemed so natural. And they had a perfect name already, with Jen having chosen the first name and Marc choosing the middle name, after his grandfather. They were ready to have this baby. August couldn't come soon enough. But something else came first.

*****

A horrible, searing pain woke Jennifer late one night in June. She felt as though she were being stabbed right in the middle of her chest. Marc called the doctor, who advised them to go to the hospital's labor and delivery department in case the baby was in distress. Tests and exams revealed nothing and the doctors chalked it up to acid reflux—not an uncommon occurrence during pregnancy—and sent Jen home with a "fancified" version of Maalox. She finally drifted back off to sleep, grateful the pain had subsided and praying she'd never feel that bad again.

Just a few weeks later, a repeat performance landed them right back at the hospital. The stabbing sensation was back in full force despite the prescription medication. Again, the hospital staff monitored the baby—his heartbeat was strong and normal. He was fine. It was Jen they had to worry about.

Other episodes occurred semi-regularly, not always enough to warrant a hospital visit, but enough to concern both Marc and Jennifer. She kept telling herself that as soon as she had the baby, the acid reflux would go away and she wouldn't have to deal with it anymore. She just had to put up with it for a couple more months.

In the meantime, there were plans to be made. Friends threw baby showers, both sets of parents scheduled visits to coincide with the due date so they could assist. Jen kept up with work and the added activity as best she could, despite the morning sickness that still plagued her and the ever-present fatigue of being both very pregnant *and* anemic. *It will all be worth it once I hold my beautiful baby boy,* she thought over and over.

✳✳✳✳✳

Monday, 6:30 am. It was her first day of maternity leave. Jennifer had decided to take a few days off until the baby arrived and use them to rest and shore up her energy for the round-the-clock feedings that waited for her just around the bend. Her due date wasn't for two more days, and everyone told her that first babies are usually late, so she figured she had a little time to get ready.

Dodging the cat, Jen made her way sleepily to the bathroom and pulled down her pajama bottoms just as her water broke. She called out to Marc, already taking a shower, and he went into action, calling the doctor and their parents in quick succession. The doctor told them to be at his office at eight, and the pair felt giddy as the realization hit them: they were going to have a baby, and *soon*.

At the doctor's office, they got the confirmation that Jen's water had, indeed, broken (after she again pulled down her pants and flooded the floor while changing into a dressing gown). She wasn't having any contractions yet, so they weren't sent to the hospital. Instead, they were advised to go home and walk as much as possible to help bring labor on.

✳✳✳✳✳

"Come on, buddy, it's time," they coaxed the baby while they walked outside. The August heat was unbearable but Jen plodded along, pushing herself to keep moving despite the humidity that made her feel as though she were breathing through a soaking-wet wool blanket. "Hey, baby, today could be your birthday!" they teased. Their spirits were higher than the thermometer. They were soon to become *parents*. It still seemed a bit like a dream, despite the experiences of the past nine months.

"Any second thoughts?" Jen asked as she stopped to catch her breath.

"About the baby?" Marc asked. "It's a little late now, isn't it?"

"No, silly. About the name. We still have time to change it."

"I love it, and it suits him."

"How do you know?" she said, laughing. "We haven't even met him yet."

"I just know."

"I wish I'd feel a contraction or something, so I'd know something is happening. This is maddening." Jen brushed her hair back resolutely and started walking again.

"Maybe you've just made it too comfortable in there. He doesn't want to move out," Marc joked.

"Well then, he needs to start paying rent, or it's time to kick him out!"

Jen knew she wouldn't be able to make it much farther, so the two slowly made their way back inside to wait in the comfort of the air conditioning.

*****

The doctor had advised them to come to the hospital at noon, unless the contractions had started before then. They hadn't. Jen and Marc triple-checked the hospital bag. They ate breakfast, trying to consider what foods would best help Jennifer keep her strength up for the marathon that was about to begin. And then, they waited, watching the clock. It was a special kind of agony—this no-man's land between not yet being parents and being able to hold their baby. Sweet anticipation, pure excitement and never-ending time. At last it was time to head to the hospital. They were ready for the next chapter in their lives to begin. As it turns out, the next chapter wasn't quite on the same page.

*****

Monday, 12:15 pm. "Okay, we're going to hook you up to this monitor, which'll let us keep track of your contractions," the nurse said. "Have you been having any contractions this morning?"

And just as the nurse asked, Jen felt a tightening in her abdomen that pulled it as taut as a basketball. "I think I'm having one right now!" she said, and sure enough, the monitor confirmed it.

Marc settled himself in the chair next to Jen and watched the activity in the room, desperately glad it wasn't him lying in that bed. He marveled at his wife—so calm and so strong. And so beautiful. He wasn't sure how he'd been so incredibly lucky to have found her. He knew the odds of anyone else having stood by him through his transition were slim, and he said a silent "thank you" to whoever could hear him for the fact that she had.

The doctor breezed in to check on Jennifer. He explained that they were going to give her Pitocin, a drug that would help move labor along. "Once your water breaks, we really like to get the baby out within 24 hours to decrease the chances of infection," he explained. Jen agreed without hesitation. They were the professionals, and she was completely comfortable putting her baby's and her own life in their hands. They nurse hooked up a Pitocin drip to her IV and once again, Marc and Jen settled in to wait.

***** *

Monday, 6:00 pm. "Hi! How's my girl?" Cindy asked.

Her question was followed immediately by one from Jen's dad, who asked, "Where's my grandson?"

Jen's parents arrived from Maryland, excited to meet their first grandchild. Their arrival was a welcome relief from the monotony of waiting. The contractions were happening regularly: not too painful yet, but definitely increasing in frequency and intensity. It had been a long six hours of waiting, and both Marc and Jen were glad to have company. Jen's mom held a bouquet of flowers, while her father carried a blue balloon as he entered.

"How are you feeling, honey?" her mom asked Jen.

"I'm doing okay, thanks. Just ready for this to move along."

"I remember when you were born..." Her mom retold the story of Jennifer's birth, happy to be able to share it with her daughter at this moment. It was a pleasant way to pass the time, and it helped take Jen's mind off the now-stronger contractions. The family chatted for a couple of hours, making small talk and telling stories before the pain started to get the best of Jennifer. When the nurse came in to check and see how far she'd progressed, Jen was only 2.5 centimeters dilated. But the pain was steadily increasing, and Jen took the opportunity to request an epidural.

***** *

Monday, 8:00 pm. The anesthesiologist ushered her parents out of the room and explained the procedure: Jen would bend over the bed and a long needle would be inserted into her spinal fluid. The anesthetic would numb her from the waist down to help control the pain. Jennifer struggled to move herself into the desired position, fighting both her very pregnant belly and her very painful contractions as she did so. Unfortunately, the anesthesiologist had a difficult time locating the right spot; it took three tries to get the needle correctly positioned, but the pain relief was swift and worth it. Jennifer relaxed.

Tuesday, 1:00 am. "You're ready." She'd finally dilated to 10 cm, and the nurse called the doctor to begin. Marc stood by Jennifer's head, holding her hand, ready to offer encouragement. For her part, Jennifer felt pretty good—the pain was controlled, and she was ready to do what she needed to meet her baby. The next hour was a blur of "Push," "Relax," "Let's try again," and "Okay, now!" Marc counted with her each time, one to ten, before she'd rest and then start again. It was a long sixty minutes that yielded nothing. The baby wasn't progressing.

The nurse leaned over Jennifer with a cool, damp cloth and wiped her forehead. "Why don't we take a break? Get some rest, and we'll give this another shot in a bit."

Jennifer slumped back in the bed. She was tired, but more than that, she was defeated. All of that work and the baby hadn't moved. Marc was exhausted too. While he wasn't doing the pushing, he was expending every bit of energy he had to encourage his wife. Jen closed her eyes and tried to doze.

Marc took advantage of her comfort to rest as well, knowing he was going to need his strength in the hours to come. He stretched out in the chair and promptly fell asleep.

*****

Tuesday, 2:30 am. "Ready to try again?" the nurse asked as she came back in, the doctor right behind her.

"Sure. Let's do this!" Jen was eager to comply. Marc, however, was sound asleep. "Marc? Marc!" His eyes remained closed.

The nurse padded over and physically shook him. At last his eyes opened slowly. "Would you like to have a baby now?" the nurse quipped.

Marc smiled sheepishly. "I guess I dozed off." He stood and resumed his position next to Jen, yawning as he did so. Jen smiled at shook her head at him. She would've teased him, but it was time to focus.

"And here we go. Push!" the nurse instructed.

It felt like the first time: trying, resting, pushing again. Encouragement, sweat, exhaustion, and ultimately, defeat. The baby wasn't coming out.

*****

Jen dropped back on the pillows, sweaty, exhausted and frustrated.

She'd been pushing for three and a half hours, and they'd gotten nowhere.

The doctor spoke up. "Mrs. Wyndham, I think we need to consider a C-section at this point."

It was the last thing they wanted to hear, but it didn't come as a surprise. The baby's heart rate had started dropping sporadically. It came back up each time Jennifer changed position, but it was an early indication that he wasn't happy, and they weren't taking chances. Exhausted, Jen and Marc signed the form. Their baby was about to be born.

*****

Tuesday, 6:00 am. Marc looked like a Hazmat worker. Covered from head to toe in protective gowning, he was escorted into the operating room. Jen was already on the operating table, and nurses were strapping her arms down. The restraints felt cold and only upped her anxiety. *It isn't supposed to be this way,* she thought, as they clamped her wrist. She got to give Marc a quick glance before they dropped a sheet right in front of her face, where it brushed her nose and blocked her view of the lower half of her body. Nervous, claustrophobic, and scared, Jen felt powerless.

The anesthesiologist stood by her head, ensuring she was still numb from the epidural. Marc was hidden somewhere on the other side of the drape, out of Jennifer's line of sight but able to watch as the doctors prepared to bring his son into the world. Time seemed to speed up and stop all at once.

*****

Tuesday, 6:20 am. It was taking a long time, longer than it should have. *It should have been just a few minutes, what's wrong?* Jennifer's mind imagined the worst. No one was saying anything. An enormous pressure on her chest. *Is someone sitting on me? What the hell is happening?* Her hysteria grew, and she knew she was going to vomit. Turning her head at the last moment, she threw up into her hair as the pressure on her abdomen increased. Someone was sobbing. Was it her? The nurse, trying to give her sedatives. *WHAT IS HAPPENING?*

And then the pressure in her chest stopped but the room broke into chaos. Extra staff rushed in. So many people.

"Elliott!" Jennifer called out.

"He isn't breathing," Jen heard someone say.

"This isn't happening, this isn't happening," Jennifer repeated over and over.

The medical team went to work. The baby's heart had stopped. CPR was started.

"This isn't happening." Jen whispered again, the drape still blocking her view.

Marc watched wide-eyed across the room as the nurses worked on his son. The anesthesiologist looked at him, taking in his shock and fear. "I'm sorry I can't give you something to help you feel better, too." A nurse in pink scrubs tried to catch his eye, urging him to relax, trying to communicate things would be okay. Marc thought he might faint.

"This isn't happening," Jen repeated over and over, like a prayer.

"He's breathing!" A nurse said, and Jen took her first breath in what seemed like forever. Her son was breathing. He was alive.

*****

Tuesday, 6:40 am. The doctors needed to close Jen up, so Marc followed as the medical team took the baby out of the room. Jennifer, exhausted and unsure of what was happening, lay on the table as the doctor sutured her abdomen. The pressure she'd felt was the team trying to pull the baby out. He'd tried to descend, after all, and was stuck far down in the birth canal. They'd had to force him back up before they could pull him out of her. The sutures complete, the nurse wheeled Jennifer into recovery, where she waited, terrified, for news of her son. She hadn't even seen him yet.

*****

Tuesday, 7:30 am. Marc came in quietly, in case Jennifer was sleeping. But she was wide awake and waiting to hear something—anything—about the baby.

"He's okay," Marc said immediately, so she would know. "But they're going to take him over to UVA medical center because they're better prepared to care for him there."

"Can I see him first?" Jen asked, in tears. "Please, I need to see him!"

The door opened and a kindly nurse wheeled in what looked like an oversized microwave oven. It was a travel incubator, and inside, hooked up to untold numbers of wires, was her son. Elliott. He was sleeping, eyes closed and looking like an angel. She drank in the sight of him. Her baby. Already gone from her mind was the pain of his birth, the contractions, the pushing, the morning sickness. All she could see was his face and her future.

His hand was free of the blanket that warmed him, and Jennifer reached out to touch it—scarcely daring to believe he was real. Her fingers brushed his, and his eyes opened. He looked right at her, a knowing, wise, age-old glance that spoke volumes without a word. Her son. They wheeled the incubator out, and Jen fell back against the pillows. Exhausted. Terrified. In love.

*****

The next few days were a blur for both of them. Jennifer had lost a lot of blood in delivery, and coupled with her already anemic body, she struggled to regain her strength. The C-section had taken its toll on her, and she spent much of each day resting.

Marc, on the other hand, was on the go nonstop. He traveled back and forth between hospitals, visiting the baby and then driving to visit his wife. His updates were the highlights of Jen's day, and she waited anxiously for any news of how Elliott was doing. Jen's mom and dad visited, keeping her company and helping her pass the time. Friends stopped by her hospital room, bringing flowers and stuffed animals and well wishes. It would've been a wonderful bonding time if only she'd been able to see her son. The hole in her heart was cavernous.

It was Friday before Jen was released from the hospital, and she waited eagerly in her wheelchair at the hospital entrance for Marc to pull up the car. *I'm coming, little one, I'm coming!* she thought, as she tapped her foot on the wheelchair's footrest. *Mommy's on her way!* With an assist into the car and a wave from the nurse, they were off—leaving one hospital behind on their way to another, where their son was waiting.

*****

Saturday night, Jennifer got to hold her future in her arms for the very first time. Still attached to wires and monitors, Elliott was tethered to within an inch of his life, but the feeling of holding her baby for the first time was the sweetest moment she'd ever known. She inhaled his scent, filling her nose and her very soul with the fragrance of her child. She was certain no one had ever been so in love with a human being as she was with him. Her son.

Little Elliott had been so sick because he'd suffered from Hypoxic Ischemic Encephalopathy, or HIE, a brain dysfunction that results from too little oxygen during birth. Doctors had been treating him with hypothermia treatments, cooling his brain in an attempt to reverse any damage. Specialists explained to the weary couple that they couldn't be sure how it might affect Elliott's development down the road. He would have to be seen regularly by a developmental specialist for the first two years to watch for any cognitive issues and neurodevelopmental delays.

Elliott wasn't released for another six days, but at last, Jennifer and Marc could bring him home and start their lives together. The nursery they'd prepared, the clothes they'd laid out, the diapers neatly stacked by the changing table—it had all been there waiting, ready to be put to use. And finally, it was. They walked through the apartment door, and it was no longer an apartment. It felt different. It felt fuller, livelier. Lovelier. It felt like a home.

*****

The next few weeks went smoothly, or as smoothly as they could with a newborn in the mix. Mother and father quickly got up to speed on changing diapers and feedings every three hours. Days and nights blurred, along with their sense of the outside world. Marc and Jennifer enjoyed cocooning with their little family, venturing out when necessary but preferring to hunker down in their nest together in bleary-eyed bliss.

When she awoke with a start, it wasn't because the baby was fussing. It was the pain—the stabbing, searing pain she'd felt before. The acid reflux was back, but this was the worst yet. Jen gasped at the indescribable agony and woke Marc. "I need to go to the hospital," she managed before another wave of pain hit. Sleep-deprived and not yet comprehending, Marc tried to make his brain cooperate. "What's wrong? Elliott?"

"No," Jen expelled the word like it was a weight. "It's me. The pain is back."

Marc pulled himself together and stumbled into the nursery, fumbling with the light and the tiny snaps to get the baby dressed. He could still hear Jen moaning in the other room as he fixed a bottle and strapped the baby in the car carrier. The three of them headed back to the hospital, uncertain of what was going on but knowing it was something serious.

*****

The scene was familiar: the crowded waiting room, the florescent lights, the disembodied voice over the loudspeaker paging this nurse or that doctor. The only difference this time was the tiny infant that came along for the ride, sleeping peacefully while his mother writhed in agony. Even the diagnosis was the same: acid reflux, but the follow-up directions changed this time. They instructed Jen to see her primary care physician, since the reflux should have subsided when she gave birth. And when she got in for her doctor's appointment, Jennifer finally got her answer: the root cause of the pain she'd had all these months was not acid reflux at all. She had gallstones. Not only that, but in her particular case, they'd caused pancreatitis.

Not all gallstones require automatic surgery. Given Jennifer's recent C-section, the doctor suggested waiting to see whether the issue would resolve itself without intervention. Two more visits to the ER over the next several weeks confirmed that wasn't going to happen; she'd have to have her gallbladder removed.

Surgery was scheduled for December 29th, but, as is life's way, things don't always happen on schedule. Jen woke up the day after Christmas, vomiting violently. As had become their routine, Marc packed up the baby, and the three of them trooped to the ER together. This time, the waiting room was jam-packed with victims suffering from a rampant case of the flu that was making the rounds. While Jen wailed in pain, Marc went in search of something she could use to throw up in. When it was clear that she'd be waiting awhile due to the sheer volume of patients in front of her, a nurse came and drew blood on her in the waiting room so her blood work could be performed while she waited. The wait was unbearable—eighteen hours before a room was available. The blood work confirmed she was having a gallbladder attack and another round of pancreatitis. In fact, the two organs were so inflamed they had to pump Jen full of antibiotics and wait for the inflammation to subside before they could take her in to surgery. Marc and Elliott sat by her side, waiting, as the pain meds finally brought her some relief. At last the nurse came to take her to surgery. The dreaded gallbladder was removed. With the source of the pain gone, Jen felt immediate relief in recovery. It was the end of a very long episode.

Chapter 16
Beyond the Picket Fence

It is Wednesday, which means it's trash day. *Great*, Jen thinks. *I bet Marc forgot to put the can out again.* The thought comes with no judgment, no malice. She knows her husband well. After ten years of marriage, she doesn't expect him to remember, simply because she hadn't remembered to remind him. No worries. The truck will come around again on Saturday.

She is newly awake, and her mind flashes through the day's schedule as it does each morning. Sneak downstairs before the kiddo wakes and get the coffee going. Then back upstairs to wake up Marc, who's harder to rouse as his body combats the sleep apnea that's worsened over the past few years. Get the dog out for a walk and pull herself together to be out the door by 6:00 for work.

It's a routine that is as predictable as the calendar, and yet, this particular morning, she finds herself musing about it. The consistency of it all doesn't bother her. In fact, she savors it in some way—knowing how the morning will unfold.

Marc will get the baby up, get him dressed, and get breakfast together. It sounds simple enough, but Jen knows the seeming simplicity can be deceiving depending on Elliott's mood. After all, he's a toddler, with all that entails—independence, defiance, and all the "I'll-do-it-my-own-self"-ness that comes along with the realization that one is nearly three years old and needs to prove his capabilities. Elliott's early medical trauma has not caused any developmental delays. He is as healthy and feisty as any other kid his age, and Jen gives thanks for that often.

Jen yawns, stretches and sits up on the edge of the bed, feet brushing the rug beneath them. As she stands, she catches a glimpse of herself in the full-length mirror that hangs on the front the bathroom door. Running her hands down her sleep shirt, she takes in her figure. She's fuller than she'd like to be, the days of anorexia long gone but the self-loathing never too far below the surface. She's still trying to accept her own body the way she has

Marc's. Jen recalls the awful darkness that enveloped her back then. She doesn't dwell on it: it's past. But it's there just the same, a part of her life that helped her to get where she is today.

And where, exactly, is she? Home. Living a life she adores and wouldn't change for the world, even if it meant reliving all of the hell to get here. Because she's happy. She truly is. Which is kind of a miracle, when she thinks about it. During those black days—the days of splitting her skin and starving herself—she never would've imagined she'd feel joy again. And yet, she does. And she refuses to take it for granted.

Hard to imagine life being any different, she thinks, slipping on her socks and padding quietly downstairs. Marc said the same thing not too long ago. One night after they got Elliott to bed, the conversation took a philosophical turn. She'd asked Marc how he thinks his life might've been different if he'd been born a male, or if he'd transitioned earlier. His response stopped her in her tracks. "I'd have been happier with my body sooner, for sure. But I never would've had you. If I'd already been a man, you wouldn't have been attracted to me. We never would've been us."

We never would've been us.

As she flicks on the coffee pot (*that* part, at least, she'd remembered to prepare last night), she wonders briefly what she'd be doing if Marc hadn't ever been part of her life. If she were still married to Marika, a queer couple with a baby. She'd thought that so often in those early days—of the life she'd dreamed of and was denied. Two moms, walking their baby through the park, facing life and its triumphs and challenges together. That thought had consumed her so often in the first several months, and each time, she felt again as though her future had been ripped away from her. Looking back on it, she realizes how much wasted energy she'd expended wondering, "*What if?*"

It was a game Marc liked to play in the early days of their relationship: he'd ask ridiculous questions that didn't require an answer but were fun to consider. "What if a meteor hit that table over there?" "What if that guy is actually a gang banger in disguise and he's gonna rob us?"

What if?

What if Marc had never transitioned? What if he'd never shared his authentic self with Jen? Jennifer would be married to someone who'd likely be desperately unhappy. Or maybe they wouldn't have made it at all; Marc feeling confined, unfulfilled, and unable to accept himself, probably wouldn't have been able to find joy in living a life that amounted to a lie. As Jen watches Marc these days, being a father to their son and a husband to her, she realizes she couldn't imagine her life any other way.

Why would she? She has a beautiful, healthy child who makes every day a blessing. Like all mothers, she marvels at his intellect, certain he's the most brilliant boy who ever lived. She studies his eyelashes as he snuggles up next to her when they watch TV in the evening, and her heart sings when he belly-laughs at Marc pretending to be a dinosaur. She imagines him heading off to kindergarten on the first day, unabashedly climbing up the steps to the bus or maybe unwilling to let go of her leg at the bus stop as other parents look on with sympathetic, knowing smiles. Jen has even thought about dancing with her son on his wedding day—sentimental about an event that's ages away but that she knows will be upon her in the blink of an eye.

She watches her own mother thrill at being "Grandma," and thinks how Cindy refers to Marc as Elliott's "daddy" without thinking twice about it. Her circle of love—her circle of family—feels complete.

For a long time after Elliott was born, Jennifer was certain they'd only have one child; the idea of going through nine months of morning sickness followed by the drama of another labor and delivery was more than she was willing to entertain. But just recently they've tentatively discussed it, thinking maybe one more child would complete their family.

She can see it, almost as though it were a painting in front of her: the four

of them, playing Frisbee in the yard or racing each other down a waterslide on a phantom summer vacation somewhere. Maybe she'd have a girl this time, and Jen would buy her first pair of ballet shoes and help her learn to put on makeup. Jennifer would watch as her son protected her daughter against everything from bullies to the boogeyman, he alone allowed to pick on his sister or call her names.

And then their children grow up. Maybe marry. Hopefully decide to have children of their own. Jen can picture that, too—she and Marc as the coolest grandparents ever. Even now, with their son not even three, they sometimes spy an old couple out and about and look at each other with a soft smile, each knowing the other is thinking the same thing: *that's gonna be us someday.* Jennifer envisions the two of them years from now, sitting on the same side in a booth at IHOP for the early-bird special. Marc would be wearing sandals with his socks pulled up to his kneecaps and she would sport a bright ribbon in her hair and an oversized straw bag filled with an assortment of blood pressure medicine, coupons for Golden Corral and hard candies scattered across the bottom of her bag like so many shells on the beach. Tacky to some, but to them—a colorful life meant to be embraced. *"We never would've been us."*

Jen knows at some point, they will tell their son what they know about the man who donated his sperm so that Marc and Jen could have their son. They'll also tell Elliott about Marc's transition. In fact, Marc already has, whispering his story to his son while rocking him to sleep as a newborn. But they'll tell him again when he's old enough to understand (and young enough not to tell everyone he sees in the grocery store) that his daddy used to be a girl. Jennifer smiles to herself at that. Ironic that she can smile about something that—not all that long ago—seemed like the end of her world.

It wasn't though.

In fact, she thinks, *in some ways it was just the beginning.*

Jen climbs the stairs to wake her husband.

*****

Hope

You eluded me for so long
I told myself you didn't exist
No such thing
Not for me

When I tried to cling to you
You ran from me
Skipping lightly from my grasp

It was a long, treacherous journey
But I caught up to you
I held you in my clenches for a time
Afraid you would forsake me

Now I cradle you in my arms
And I'm never letting go.

*****

Acknowledgements

This book took a small army to produce, and I'm thankful to everyone who supported it. From individual book orders to those who were willing to sponsor, from those who helped me shape it to those who helped me with the physical production of it: I'm eternally grateful.

At the risk of leaving someone out, I'm going to give a shout out to some folks who played a major part in this project.

First, to Jennifer and Marc, whose bravery in sharing their story is unparalleled. I treasure your friendship more than you'll ever know. Fate brought us together. I truly believe that, and I couldn't be more humbled that you allowed me to chronicle your journey.

To my Official Sponsors, Marjorie Adam of The Marjorie Adam Team and Debbie Kozura of Deb Kozura Photography – you both have a very special place in this project. Your support opened doors that might have forever been closed. Thank you for believing in me!

To my Word of Mouth Supporters: Bruce Follmer, Tiffany Smith of The Virginia Shop, George Christensen and Steve Kotrch, and Meredith Tupper of PintSize Graphics, your encouragement and belief in me and this project means so very much!

Several people were kind enough to invest a little more than the book price to be recognized in these pages. To you, I raise a toast:

Heather Arquitt	*Sarah Elizabeth*	*Pranava Moody*
Karen Barker	*Edwards*	*Farah Nawaz*
Julie Bivens	*Kelly Hager*	*Sharon Reichard*
Deb Booth	*Trista Haugen*	*LeeAnn Rose*
Raymond Bowers	*Ted Heck*	*Geri Schirmer*
David Costa	*Jason Hintz*	*Leonard Smallacombe*
Bob Crane	*Skip Horne*	*Mary Beth Tourbin*
Ginny and Bob Crane	*Penny Howard*	*Debe Turnbull*
Renee Deming	*Kip McCharen*	*Polly Victor*

And to all of those who supported me with individual orders in my crowdfunding campaign, each and every one of you is a rock star! That you were willing to put money up front and hope that a book that wasn't even written yet would be worth owning ... well, I'm not sure whether that makes you overly optimistic or easily hornswoggled, but either way I'm gratified you believed in me.

To Jaime Kurtz, Carmen Shenk, and H.L. Brooks, thanks for lifting this fellow author up, sharing insights, and taking the journey with me. Here's to all of us making it on the NY Times Bestseller List!

To Maria at Mascot Books, I'm so glad you took a chance on this book! To my project manager, Kristin, thank you for walking me through the process. To Heidi, thank you for your eagle eye and insightful suggestions. Your edits made this so book much stronger!

To the awesome folks at Publishizer, my first-ever crowdfunding campaign was a great experience due to you. I'm awfully happy you exist. (Even if I didn't win the contest).

To Angie Batten, Renee Deming, Greg Rumpf and Liz Weaver—you all played various roles in the actual marketing and production of this book. Thank you from the bottom of my heart for sharing your technical and artistic expertise. Each of you is an artist, and I bow to your talents.

Speaking of artists, to my sister, Deb Booth: thank you for being next to me every step of the way. From being my own personal champion to supporting this endeavor with purchases, artwork and social media shares, I couldn't have done it without you! I'm forever indebted to you for your ongoing advocacy and your generosity in every facet.

To my parents, Sherry and Bruce: I have so much gratitude I'm not even sure where to begin. From fostering my self-confidence to supporting my endeavors, your love for me was the rock upon which I based my life. I respect, admire, and love you both so very much.

To my dear friends, Debbie Pence and Maria Paulus, thanks for always being there no matter what I need. Thank God my secrets are safe with you.

Most of all, to Mike, Zach and Corey: you all are my life. I'm beyond blessed.

About the Author

Lynn Thorne is an award-winning writer and the author of *Word Of Mouth Advertising Online and Off: How to Spark Buzz, Excitement and Free Publicity for Your Business or Organization With Little or No Money* (Atlantic Press, 2008). As a freelance journalist, her work has appeared in *The Washington Post Express*, *The Washington Post Southern Maryland Extra*, *U.S. News Ventures*, *Access Wireless*, *Broker Agent Magazine*, and several local publications.

A former broadcast journalist, Lynn has appeared on local TV and radio stations in Virginia and Wisconsin. She received her Bachelor of Science in Mass Communications, with a specialty in Broadcasting, from Virginia Commonwealth University.

Lynn is also active on social media and is an active blogger on thatswhatlynnsaid.com, which has a primary focus on LGBT issues. She lives in Virginia with her husband and two sons.